SMOKING THE MANGO TREES

PUBLISHING

OMF International works in most East Asian countries, and among East Asian peoples around the world. It was founded by James Hudson Taylor in 1865 as the China Inland Mission. Our overall purpose is to glorify God through the urgent evangelisation of East Asia's billions, and this is reflected in our publishing.

Through our books, booklets, website and quarterly magazine, *East Asia's Billions*, OMF Publishing aims to motivate Christians for world mission, and to equip them for playing a part in it. Publications include:

- contemporary mission issues
- the biblical basis of mission
- the life of faith
- stories and biographies related to God's work in East Asia
- accounts of the growth and development of the Church in Asia
- studies of Asian culture and religion relating to the spiritual needs of her peoples

Visit our website at *www.omf.org*

Addresses for OMF English-speaking centres can be found at the back of this book.

Smoking the Mango Trees

Martin C. Haworth

Monarch
BOOKS

Mill Hill, London & Grand Rapids, Michigan

Published by Monarch Books in the UK 2002,
Concorde House, Grenville Place,
Mill Hill, London NW7 3SA.

Distributed by:
UK: STL, PO Box 300, Kingstown Broadway, Carlisle,
Cumbria CA3 0QS;
USA: Kregel Publications, PO Box 2607,
Grand Rapids, Michigan 49501.

ISBN 1 85424 594 5

British Library Cataloguing Data
A catalogue record for this book is available
from the British Library.

Cover photo: John Richards

Book design and production for the publishers by
Bookprint Creative Services
P.O. Box 827, BN21 3YJ, England.
Printed in Great Britain.

DEDICATION

To the Buhid who received and kept us as their own
and
to the memory of my nephew and godson, Richard Ensor
(1988–2001) who loved life and fought so bravely

CONTENTS

LIST OF ILLUSTRATIONS

ACKNOWLEDGEMENTS

I wish to express my gratitude to the spiritual father of the Buhid, Bob Hanselman, who assisted in providing the background history to this account, and to Eve Noble for her encouragement in checking through the manuscript.

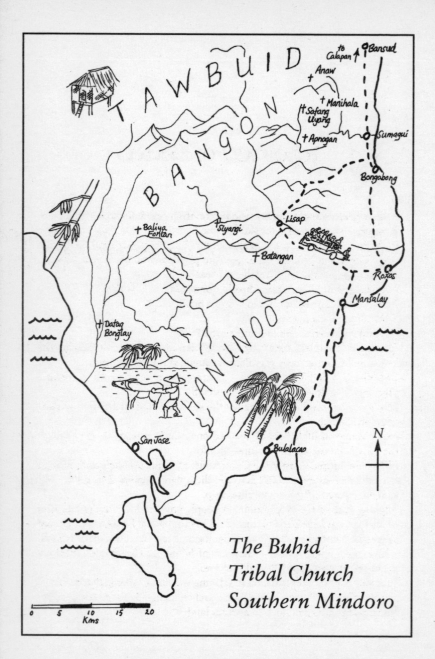

The Buhid
Tribal Church
Southern Mindoro

GLOSSARY OF TERMS

Aswang A lesser spirit being whose bite brings mortal illness.

Bangon A sub group of the Buhid tribe.

El Niño The time of drought that occurs at intervals around the Pacific Rim. This often produces the opposite phenomenon of the *La Niña*, a season of heavy rains during the dry season.

Faduwasay Buhid, meaning brother or sister.

Fangablang The most ferocious spirit being.

Fotol Buhid for a machete.

Hanunoo The tribe to the south of the Buhid.

Iglesia ni Cristo ("Church of Christ") An indigenous cult denying the Lordship of Christ, very prevalent throughout the Philippines.

Luktanon A Buhid term used in Batangan to refer to all non-tribal Filipinos, Tagalogs and Visayans especially.

Mangyan The collective name for the six indigenous tribes that inhabit Mindoro Island.

MBS Mangyan Bible School, located one hour's journey from Calapan, the provincial capital of Oriental Mindoro.

NPA New People's Army, the Communist rebel group operating through much of the Philippines and active in the upland areas of Mindoro.

OMF Overseas Missionary Fellowship.

Tagalog One of the most dominant people groups in the Philippines who occupy central Luzon Island, including Manila. When English was rejected as the one-time national language, Tagalog took its place, although this is still a language foreign to a small majority of Filipinos. The Tagalog-speaking people inhabit much of lowland Mindoro.

Visayan A large people group inhabiting the many islands that form the central section of the Philippines archipelago. Many of the poorer Visayans came to Mindoro to acquire land.

Bamboo clump

THE STRAITS OF MINDORO

Rusty steamboat unhurriedly plies the Mindoro Straits
Parting the tropic blue of a limpid sea –
Mount Halcon never seems to draw nearer
Nor the departed shores of Luzon appear to diminish
As we are caught chugging somewhere out in the straits,
Unperturbed, content in this suspension
Of having left and not yet having arrived,
Savouring a journey that keeps to no schedule.

Somewhere on this sun-filled, surreal voyage
An island is anticipated, approached, then passed;
A luxuriant hill of wind-combed cogon
And ecstatic coconut palms stretch all ridge long.
The swell breaks white, silent from the ship,
Upon the reef and cliffs of the shore,
The monotonous leagues of sea interrupted
Only for a brief entrancing while.
The island captivates our gaze, filling our thoughts,
Each ravine minutely observed
With its fascinating tangle of rampant jungle.
Fishermen's homes, gaily-painted blue, yellow and green
Were all remembered long after their passing from sight.

And the waves that washed the white sands
And the steady sea breeze in the palms along the shore
Haunted the mind all the remainder long
Of that carefree crossing to another world
Far from the frantic frenzy and sordid shanties of Manila,
Adrift and spellbound with a people not in a hurry,
Smoking, smiling, breast-feeding, chatting
Enjoying the simplicity of very few distractions.

CHAPTER ONE

THE CONVICTION

Waydinan looked out on Mount Sumagui, across the Talsi river valley. It rose bold and precipitous in parts from the gentler, lower slopes cleared for maize and rice and an assortment of citrus trees. Those lower slopes had been tamed, sweeping with gentle undulations, with here and there the appearance of a tribal hut amidst a grove of coconuts. But higher up, where the virgin rain forest was still preserved, people did not live. Not even the loggers had gone that far in spite of the giant mahogany still growing there; it was deemed too inaccessible to viably extract the fine timber and too cold for the Buhid to live.

Waydinan pondered the scene rather absent-mindedly, having grown up and spent most of his life looking out across at Mount Sumagui from his birthplace of Apnagan. Because it was familiar, there was something comforting about the aspect, the well-known pacifying the uncertainties unsettling him. His son-in-law, Gaynop, shortly joined him, squatting down on top of the grassy verge rising from the path. The path was deeply rutted by the karusas, the sledge-like carriers pulled by water buffalo, whose runners carved their course deep into the earth and scarred the hillsides.

"Will you be taking bananas down to Nara tomorrow?" asked Gaynop in his warm, gentle voice.

"Probably!" replied the older man, in a detached tone, his brow still furrowed as he looked out distantly across the valley.

"I don't know if I will be selling or not," remarked Gaynop as he examined the blade of his "fotol", the Buhid machete.

"Have you not gathered any?"

"No. But Mahay said she would bring some back with her today from our Talsi land."

"I don't suppose it will be very many!"

Gaynop nodded knowingly to his father-in-law's remark. Mahay – his wife – was not that strong, often sickly and couldn't carry a full woman's load. The two men continued at some length, talking about the day-to-day concerns of a Mindoro hill farmer.

"We need a missionary!" exclaimed Waydinan after a lengthy pause.

Gaynop made no reply. His attention was fixed, with exacting scrutiny, on his leg as he shaved away some loose itchy skin with the blade of his fotol.

"If we had a missionary," continued Waydinan positively, "we would be as one in the church. As it is now, each has his own idea and no one will follow the other. We agree in our talking, come up with our proposals, but when it comes to doing anything about it, we have lost interest! No one is prepared to follow another."

"You are probably right," acknowledged the younger man.

"What has it been – four, five years since Roberto and Ligaya left us? Look at us, the mission over west at Datag Bonglay has come to an abrupt end. The church we started across the Talsi has been taken over by others who had the money and the resources to persuade them away. Our own church has lost interest, so many are no longer committed to coming to the meetings, even on a Sunday morning. People are full of gossip and slander, a brother is not willing to forgive another for some small sin. Why, some are not even talking to one another anymore and no one is prepared to approach them about such matters and have it sorted out as we should!"

"Yes, it was better when Roberto and Ligaya were with us. Back then when we had our elders' meetings, most of the folk that were supposed to come, came. Now, how many were we earlier in our elders' meeting?"

Roberto and Ligaya referred to Bob and Joy Hanselman whose Christian names had been transposed, in Bob's case, into a Filipino equivalent, while Joy's name had been translated into Tagalog, the national language of the Philippines. Bob and Joy had spent their entire working lives among the Buhid, and were regarded as parents in the Lord.

The two men recited the names of those who had been present in the two day meetings, forcibly bending back their strong fingers of hardened and cracked skin with the other hand, counting off each individual.

"Aye, we were almost entirely from Apnagan. Only Monay came from Batangan. No one as usual came from Siyangi!"

"Bagaw came from Manihala," Gaynop added in his conciliatory way.

"Yes, but only for half a day. He was off as soon as he got his buffalo back from Onan!"

Gaynop nodded his assent, as he started to scrape at the other leg with the long, keen blade. Then he looked up.

"We could ask that new white guy, who stays in Calapan, whether they could send us a missionary!" he suggested.

"What's his name?"

"Er . . . Er . . ." Gaynop was pronouncing the first syllable of the foreigner's name, but he could not remember the rest of

"Ernesto's" name, leader of the tribal missionary team at OMF's Mindoro base at the provincial capital, Calapan.

"Never mind. Do you mean that tall missionary who rides about on a motorbike?"

"What do you mean, tall – they are all tall! Remember Roberto? I only came up to here on him," laughed Gaynop, touching below his own shoulder. Gaynop's face screwed up like a child as he smiled infectiously, accompanied by a deep, chesty laugh. Only the glummest would not respond to his playful humour. Among the Buhid Christians, it would be rare to find such a morose individual, for they have an appealing joviality.

"Yes, it would be good to ask if there is a missionary family who could come and live with us," continued Waydinan in his somewhat high voice, thin with age.

"I doubt there would be a family. It seems that most of the missionaries are unmarried women!"

"No, we should have a family," insisted the old man.

"Why's that?"

"Look at what happened when the two single missionaries came to Batangan – they didn't last a week."

"But if there are any spare missionaries, they would most likely be unmarried women," reasoned Gaynop, who by now had sheathed his fotol and was growing animated by the subject. "Besides, Miss Barham was also an unmarried woman and she was the first to come to us with the Good News."

"Miss Barham was the first," agreed Waydinan wistfully. "I suppose if it wasn't for Miss Barham we would still be living in darkness. She was the one who first brought us God's word." Waydinan paused, furrowing his brow again as he attempted to explain his inner conviction on this matter. "But we need a married couple to come as missionaries, ones who would understand marital problems, ones who would be a good example, to get alongside those who struggle and are tempted to take other spouses!"

"I agree," assented Gaynop, "but like I said, most missionaries are unmarried women." Here he paused with a roguish glint in his eye: "But maybe if we got a young one, perhaps she could marry one of our own men!" Gaynop shook with laughter. The suggestion seemed quite absurd.

Waydinan smiled, but only briefly.

The sun had begun its fast descent over the western hills. The shadows were perceptibly lengthening down in the Talsi valley, and the softer light came in broad shafts through the voluminous clouds, illuminating the humid air and magnifying mountain and jungle. The shadow, by this time, had engulfed Waydinan and Gaynop. The two men rose and headed for their homes before nightfall, to help prepare the fire to cook the evening meal, or to check on their buffalo, or to draw water from the spring: whatever needed doing.

That evening, once the elders had gathered a final time and had been satisfied with their meals of boiled rice and vegetable stew, Waydinan spoke with conviction of their need for a missionary family. After the initial, cautionary observations from others about the unlikelihood of there being such a family free, the Spirit of the Lord brought the conviction on them all that this was needed for the Buhid Church at this very time. They prayed aloud simultaneously and with deliberation, not as so often, searching for things to pray about and being excessively wordy so that no one should finish praying long before the others and so appear in an unfavourable light. No, this time they prayed with a confidence that was not their own.

Diokno noted down on a grubby, torn piece of paper, this final resolution that the elders had reached. They would approach OMF (Overseas Missionary Fellowship) with the request for a missionary family. Diokno would go to Calapan in the morning to speak with the tall one who rides a motorbike.

This item concluded the other four already listed on the page. This scrap of paper, torn a day earlier from his daughter's school jotter, had since been handled by hands more used to tending the fields and was now dirtied by fire ash and charred wood. The paper recorded the minutes of the meeting, in a fashion learned from the foreigners.

*   *   *

The cocks began crowing hesitantly quite some time before dawn, far too soon for those who were light sleepers. But for those who had a long journey to make, or had to be off for an early start to attend school down in the lowlands, it was their signal to arise and kindle the fire that was to cook the sweet potato for breakfast. Diokno was up then, groping about in his tribal hut with a poor light guttering and smoking badly. The wick was made from a twisted old cloth drawn through a hole in a lid, which rested on top of an old baked bean tin filled with paraffin. He packed a small bag with his best clothes: a faded pair of jeans, unstained from banana sap or the like, and a clean, unironed T-shirt. The darkness was intensified within the hut by the smokiness of the fire, there being no chimney.

His wife, Belen, dished up the sweet potato and from another pot served the boiled leaf tops from the sweet potato plant. The ladle Belen used was made from half a coconut shell fastened by a thin section of vine to a bamboo handle. The simple meal was served into plastic bowls, grubby with grease and fingers blackened by fire, sap and field. Diokno gave thanks and they set into their meal with deliberation whilst their children remained asleep.

Diokno went with Monay down the trail, now in the half dark just before dawn. Monay had wanted an early start too, to return to his own village of Batangan, two jeepney trips and two walks away. They spoke little on the trail, moving with determination, barefoot over the smooth boulders that provided relief from time to time from the wet clay. The clay was treacherously slippery, especially where it was steep. It was steep most of the first part of the way. But they moved with dexterity and agility, making their way without apparent effort through the squelchy, ankle-deep clay, down the mountain from Apnagan. No one else was yet on the trail, but there would be many later. Monay and Diokno hoped to arrive at the trading post at the edge of the plain, before the appearance of the banana dealers coming from the coastal towns of Bongabong and the nearer Bansud. The silvery blue of the South China Seas glimmered enticingly through the fronds of the many banana trees that stood in silhouette along their trail. An alimahon bird greeted the morning with its exquisite, deep-throated call, its liquid notes sounding like wine poured from a bottle. The bird waited a while before sounding off again. Diokno replied with an exact replica of the call, created by blowing into the closed bowl of his hands. The bird responded almost instantly. Diokno smiled but did not reply this time, intent on his journey.

The two men crossed the river at the end of the trail. On the far bank, they changed out of their working clothes into their best outfits before appearing in the lowland village of Nara, in the hope of reducing some of the abusive comments from the "Luktanon" (the Buhid name for all non-tribal Filipinos: Tagalogs, Visayans and Illocanos who have migrated onto Mindoro from neighbouring Filipino islands). The Luktanon superciliously raise their chins and derogatorily exclaim, "Mangyan", a term synonymous in their thinking with being dirty and uncivilised. Mangyan is the collective name referring to the indigenous six tribes on Mindoro, a Tagalog term possibly derived from the phrase "Mangmang iyan", meaning "that one is stupid!"

They boarded a "traysikel" – a motorbike with sidecar built for two – which they shared with six others from Nara. Once they reached the highway, about half an hour later, they parted company, Monay to the south while Diokno boarded a bus to Calapan to the north. Diokno, like so many others, slept a good part of the three-hour journey, as the bus sped along the long, straight roads of the hot, humid plains, criss-crossed by rice fields. The road potholed much of the way and as some sections had no asphalt, this made the journey slow. The drivers, to relieve the monotony of their work, became highly competitive, particularly when challenged by vehicles from other bus companies. This bravado helped to prevent their falling asleep behind the wheel: the stimulus of speed and skill in avoiding potholes, pedestrians and dogs meant they had to keep their wits about them.

Diokno disembarked right at the gate of the OMF office in Calapan. He felt conspicuous walking up the steep driveway, flanked by flowering hibiscus and many other shrubs that did not yield food. In under a minute, he arrived at a wooden, pavilion-like house. A couple of overfed dogs loudly greeted him, taking away the necessity to noisily clear his throat to announce his arrival. Soon someone emerged who led him to the office of the tall one who rides the motorbike. Diokno plucked up courage to ask the one showing him to the office, the name of this foreign leader. Although glad to discover Ernesto's identity, Diokno simply addressed him with the respectful "Kuya", meaning big brother. He did not use his name, as that, according to his tribal etiquette, was considered too personal between relative strangers.

The interview lasted some time, Ernesto asking after acquaintances they had in common, talking about farming matters, which Ernesto found natural since he had grown up on a farm in Switzerland. They then talked at length about general church matters, but still Diokno did not broach the subject about which he had come.

Familiar with their ways, Ernesto was not in a hurry to tease out the real matter. Only when the interview appeared to have reached its conclusion and Diokno had risen from his seat with Ernesto accompanying him to the door, did he pause.

"Would there happen to be a family who could come and live with us Buhid?" Diokno asked with a casual, take-it-or-leave-it sort of way. The question was accompanied by a short nervous laugh, disclosing his embarrassment at making the request.

"Ah, you want to know if OMF has a missionary family that can come to you?" Ernesto's voice rose in volume and warmth as he recognised the purpose of this visit. But the enthusiasm was temporary: he explained with a degree of disappointment the unlikelihood of his being able to oblige. No one was coming forward these days for tribal work, nor could anyone be spared from the existing team. To soften the blow, Ernesto added that he would very much like to visit Apnagan himself, and they discussed a couple of possible dates for such a visit.

Diokno felt no real regret as he left the OMF office. The Buhid had said as much themselves the previous evening in their elders' meeting, reasoning that it would be extremely unlikely there would be a family available immediately. But nevertheless he felt somewhat flat, because in spite of their reasoning, they had received what they understood to be a God-given confidence to ask. The previous night the elders had known a confidence of faith that led to their asking in prayer, and the faith too to make this long journey the very next day.

Although without human basis for hope, Diokno reported back to the church at the next meeting that they should continue to pray and believe God would send them what they needed. He read out the extremely brief minutes of the elders' meeting from the even worse-for-wear scrap of paper and concluded by noting the date: "September 18, 1993".

CHAPTER TWO

OF HEART AND MIND

Thick hemp ropes were cast into the water as the old rusty ferry-boat blew a sanguine hoot on its deep bellowing horn. The screws roared away, causing whirlpool commotion and the dive-for-a-piso boys to swim aside. We were away. The progress at first was only marked by inches against the wharf.

A group of twenty, mostly American, males, all dressed identically in black trousers with white shirt and tie, were standing on our deck, each with the same short, neat haircut. The identification on their black badges read "The Church of Jesus Christ and the Latter Day Saints", more simply known as Mormons, a cult who preach a very different gospel, with much added "revelation", denying the Lordship of Christ. The Mormons appeal to the Filipino with their respectable presentation, friendliness and beautiful buildings; qualities held in value in this insolvent nation.

Churchgoers here, more often than not, come from poor and incomplete homes or from squatter communities where households are often impoverished by drink, gambling and drugs. Therefore to come into a fine church building, is to enter something that is otherworldly, substantial, complete and promising hope. This appeals to material and spiritual instincts alike, and reflects the Roman Catholic background, the dominant importance and centrality of the ornate church in the main plaza of every town.

Three hours later, the rough straits of Mindoro had been crossed. The pilot was making his fourth attempt to dock the ship in a heavy swell. Our eyes scanned Calapan's near horizon. The dome of the Catholic church rose well above the rest of the unremarkable town, vying for prominence with the triple spires of the Iglesia ni Cristo, an indigenous sect well established throughout the Philippines. Practically everywhere you choose to go in this country, these two large buildings are likely to dominate the skyline. As the pilot failed to get a mooring on his fourth attempt, the ferry was tossed, with a heavy thud, onto a neighbouring ship at berth. Paul's comment came to my mind about the need for sound teaching to build up people in Christ:

"Then [they] will no longer be infants, tossed back and forth by the waves and blown here and there by every wind of teaching and by the cunning and craftiness of men in their deceitful scheming." (Eph. 4:14)

OMF have two basic initiatives on Mindoro. One was to the lowland, Roman Catholic community, and the other to the Mangyan tribes. I had made a brief trip a few months earlier, without my wife Alexandra and the children, to a Mangyan village and had left strangely warmed by the experience. An immediate bonding with these straightforward tribal folk had been apparent.

But the problem was, as I was told at the time by one respected senior missionary, that the Mangyan work no longer needed missionaries and was now in the hands of the Mangyan themselves. The only exceptions were the one or two elderly missionaries still overseeing the church until they retired.

When I had returned home all enthusiastic about that first, exotic adventure with the Mangyan up in the mountains, a trip that had so appealed to my love of the countryside and my affinity with down-to-earth people, Alexandra was alarmed. She warned: "Don't you ever think that I will become a tribal missionary!" in a quick attempt to uproot this unwelcome notion.

It brought to mind my words to Alexandra before we married: "Don't ever expect me to become a missionary!"

I am not suggesting God sadistically delights in putting us into nightmare scenarios to test the limits of our endurance. But it does highlight the need to clear the "no-go" areas in our thinking and submit these to the Lordship of Christ. The natural ability to overcome some of those deep-seated prejudices is usually beyond us, but by inviting God to deal with them through prayer, we venture out afresh with God. Grace is the very thing God provides to those who yield their prejudices to Him, submitting our rights out of reverence to follow the Master.

With that yielding, God comes with the power to change our thinking and our ways, bringing a peace where previously we had known only discomfort and resistance. Jesus said that: "Anyone who does not take up his cross and follow me is not worthy of me. Whoever finds his life will lose it, and whoever loses his life for my sake will find it." (Matt. 10:38–39). This truth can never be known or proven until we do finally yield to Him and take Him at His word. It is the picking up of our cross, the losing of our lives that brings the purpose and significance of real life, sometimes surprisingly through the very thing that previously appeared so disagreeable.

Beyond Calapan, Mount Halcon rose majestically, its 8,500-foot bulk emerging abruptly from the rice plains like an atomic explosion. We wondered for a moment whether it was real, half obscured as it was in the humid haze of the tropics. The distant summit ridge was so high that we reasoned it must be a deceiving cloud! Halcon does not stand isolated, but forms part of a long mountain range stretching from the northern shores to those of the south, in an unbroken chain, flanked on either side by fertile plains. It is in these mountains the Mangyan live, isolated from the commerce and bustle of the lowlands.

At the foot of Mount Halcon we spent part of our field trip. Having been taken on the usual round of visits to a lowland church, then the Bible College at Pinamalayan which serves the churches of the plains, and after a relaxed stay at the OMF mission home up on a small hill above the road to Calapan Pier, we were dropped off at the Mangyan Bible School near Baco at the great mountain's base. We were to be left there for three days to see how we would fare on our own, without another missionary, with only Mangyan as companions.

Alexandra had her misgivings. After all, what on earth could someone brought up on the outskirts of Manchester possibly have in common with tribal folk emerging from an Iron Age existence? I had had just a glimpse of the Mangyan, a day and a night, but it seemed considerably longer due to the richness of the experience. I wondered how Alexandra would overcome her most natural concerns.

I began to dwell upon those ridiculous "what-if?" scenarios that the natural man torments his mind with. What if Alexandra was not able to relate with these people, or cope with the most basic living conditions, without a washing machine or a househelp, without a toilet, electricity and running water?

I wrongly thought I would have to resort to some subtle persuasion so that Alexandra might yield! I did ask God to convince her, but inwardly I worried as though it all depended on my powers of persuasion. It was a ridiculous presumption, because even if I had the ability to convince my wife (which I don't in such life-changing matters), I was denying that God would call us as husband and wife, which after all was a divinely appointed calling too. If God had touched my heart with the needs of these people, He would also give a similar love and burden to Alexandra for the Mangyan.

But in all of these inward comings and goings, I had not forgotten that statement of the senior missionary that the Mangyan work was coming to an end with regard to missionary help. The superintendent (as the team leaders were known then) did not give much further hope either on this matter. We were led to believe that this stay at the tribal Bible school was just a routine part of the field trip to give an overview of OMF's work. He was cagey as to whether there were any more openings in the tribal work, but revealingly remarked that it required specialised people. Beyond that, he would say no more other than to conclude with the cryptic remark: "Anyway, go and see for yourself at the school and see how you get on!"

And so we were dropped off with our three days' supply of just-add-water noodles and dried asparagus soups, dried milk and damp sugar. Deposited at the end of a very broken track that twice forded a river, we soon reached the school. Provided with a more-than-adequate house, raised up on stilts, it differed from other tribal houses, in having a toilet and taps with running water, and electricity too! Yanigia, the school principal and his wife, Lufai, paid us a visit and were most patient with our limited language skills. In a way, it made them perhaps warm more to us, for there was nothing special about us to intimidate these shy people.

They left us to settle in and relax. Mid-afternoon, lunched and rested, we went out to mingle with the school community, who were all engaged in various chores. The men had gone off to work some distance away in their communal rice field, a scheme aimed towards self-sufficiency as well as providing a surplus to sell and cover the school's overheads. Alexandra joined the ladies sitting on logs down the slope, busy chopping away at coconuts, preparing copra. Soon equipped with a machete, she caused much hilarity, unskilfully hacking at the resistant coconut shells in an attempt to split them and gouge out the inner lining. The 16-inch blade bounced off the tough shell and stabbed the air or ground, making those nearby draw discreetly away. It was soon suggested that she might like to place the nut to dry on a bamboo shelf constructed over a smoky fire, before she did either herself or anyone else an injury.

The ice was broken and the questions began to flow; the usual kind. How many children did she have? How many had survived infancy? How long had we been married? Why did we only have two children if we had been married eight years already? Perhaps I worked away from home for much of the year?

They were all very pleased to tell her how many children they had and talked about their schooling concerns, and how far the older ones had to travel to go to high school. They spoke of their tribal villages, of absent brothers and sisters, parents; of how good the Bible school was here, and of how the Lord had called them to study for the three years. Alexandra realised their concerns were basically not very different from our own. Instead of having little or no point of reference, they had so much to talk about that the women had eventually to excuse themselves to go and prepare the supper.

Next morning our son Iain had the excitement of waking up to find the hen that had roosted on the end of his bed had laid an egg! For that to happen to a lad of six was sufficient calling to such a life. Hannah was at home too in the fresher climate up in the hills, where she was not so bothered by prickly heat. She enjoyed the long, surprisingly cool baths in the mountain river. Both our children were much relieved not to be the focus of as much adult attention as they were used to. The Luktanon enjoy interacting with children, excited to see Western children especially if they have whiter-than-usual skin, blue eyes and fair hair. But this attention almost always included much cheek pinching which, being really quite painful, challenged the patience of both child and parent. Luktanon seemed surprised when the children did not enjoy such attention and would sometimes conclude that our children were proud!

The real basis of our calling though was cemented by a trip up to Ayan Bekeg which I had visited previously without the rest of the family. Ayan Bekeg was the nearest wholly Mangyan village from the Bible school, a two- to three-hour hard trek up the lower flanks of Mount Halcon. One of the Mangyan students and the eleven-year-old daughter of the principal guided us up there. It was not just the affinity we felt with these beautifully uncomplicated people, but we saw a real need for basic Bible teaching. One of the church elders confided in us, saying that shortly after my first trip to his village, a group of Luktanon had come with an Amerikano, wanting to teach the church members and lead them on in to the full revelation of Jesus Christ.

"They said there was another book of equal importance to the Bible! They wanted to open our minds to this book, so we could be truly saved! I said that we were not interested as we have had missionaries come to us for many years who never mentioned another book as important as the Bible. Did I do right?" the elder asked, looking slightly apologetic, fearing he had sent away true brothers. He was relieved to hear our affirmation.

We began to wonder how long a church could stand under such an assault, from the Mormons in this case and from the other active cults, with the knowledge that the Bible alone is God's word? If Mangyan Christians were unable to give the reason for the confidence they had in Christ for salvation, then false teachers who persisted could probably win them over. Such thieves use persuasive words: Christ was no more than a man, a prophet, not the Almighty Lord. They deliberately confuse with their rehearsed questions and memorised scripture portions to dazzle with displays of superior knowledge.

We recalled those 20 or so Mormons, our fellow passengers just a few days earlier, bound for this same island also on a spiritual mission, but one so very different from ours. The Mormons were a militant contingent to be reckoned with, who during the 1990s supposedly sent more workers to the Philippines than to any other country.

"You know, another thing that worries me," continued the elder, warming now to our presence, "is the way that many of our Christians are returning to chanting to the spirits of the dead when someone is sick." The elder lent forward and let a great globule of saliva, reddened by betel-nut, fall accurately between the bamboo slats of the floor we were seated upon.

"Another thing," he continued, "so many of our folk don't bother coming to church anymore. How do we encourage them back again? I tell you, those who faithfully come are very discouraged, arguing with those who play basketball instead of coming to church or are away on a jaunt to the town! What is to be done and what will come of all this?" The elder shook his head and wrapped his jacket closer about him, uncomfortable as much with the climate of change as with the cool air at this altitude.

As we understood the ongoing need to strengthen these churches against the resurgent tide of pagan practices, to shore them up against the onslaught of the cults, combined with the gut feeling that here was a people we were able to relate to, and who were open with us, there came to us the call, compounded by Paul's instruction to Timothy:

> "Preach the word; be prepared in season and out of season; correct, rebuke and encourage – with great patience and careful instruction."

When I read these words from 2 Timothy 4:2, I received my commission from the Lord. These words were so impressed upon my heart that they were forever being brought to mind over the coming years as I discovered the problems of Ayan Bekeg were to be found elsewhere too. Reading on in that fourth chapter, I heeded the warning that Paul was eager to impress on this young missionary:

> "For the time will come when men will not put up with sound doctrine. Instead, to suit their own desires, they will gather around them a great number of teachers to say what their itching ears want to hear. They will turn away from the truth and turn aside to myths."

I found myself growing alarmed by the real danger these struggling churches were facing, and by the quiet desperation felt by elders unequal to the task of scriptural correction. What good would it be if 40 years of toil spent planting the Mangyan churches were to be nullified by abandoning them now to their own devices, before their time had come, and leaving them to be swept away by false teachers? The context Paul was addressing in his second letter to Timothy, the emergence of false teachers among an immature church, was not very different from the situation we found here on Mindoro.

The Lord laid all these things on our hearts in September 1993, coinciding exactly with the prayer for help from the Buhid church elders. This was no coincidence! The Buhid had called out to the Lord in faith for a missionary family and God laid on our heart and mind, through another tribal group, the very similar precarious nature of the tribal churches.

* * *

In fact God foreknew this need a long time before He called us to the Philippines, a nation we knew virtually nothing about and had little interest in. I had particularly struggled with the calling to the Philippines. I felt no empathy with its people or culture, something which I thought I should feel if I were to go.

Alexandra did not share this problem, as the Lord gave her various signs and tokens over a very limited space of time, through her meeting with a number of individuals who had recently come from the Philippines, not all of whom were connected with OMF, nor even Christian. These "chance" encounters led her to acknowledge that God was speaking very specifically to her, leading her to the point of obedience to go to the Philippines.

I remember spending a weekend at an OMF conference in Glasgow, hearing first-hand accounts of folk who had been on short-term mission exposure trips to the Philippines. Even though they showed colourful photographs and spoke graphically and with enthusiasm about their visit, I still remained untouched.

Alone on the long road home from this Glasgow conference, I wrestled with God about this calling. I had spent seven significant years amongst the Arabs and knew what it was to have a close affinity with another race. But God had kept the door closed to the Arab world and I could not understand why. Unmoved by all I had heard about the Philippines, it was with this field in mind that the OMF leadership gave us a warm welcome to come and join any one of several teams. Leaders in other fields who had read our papers did not extend this enthusiastic welcome. All this troubled and confused me as I anticipated God would relate to me in a way that He does so often with others, confirming a calling by giving an early love and burden for those He sends them to.

God spoke with me on that long drive home. Did He not love all people with an equal love? Were not all made in His image? What did man have to commend him to God when Christ gave us his life? Yet Christ loved all of us unconditionally. The only true spiritual response to these rhetorical questions was: "Yet not as I will, but as you will".

God operates in a multitude of different ways. It is quite erroneous for us to expect God to behave in a specific way, on the grounds of someone else's experience, or to limit His dealings on the basis of our own understanding of the way He guides. God is not bound by our rules. He is the Lord and deals with us as individuals.

But I would observe that guidance most often comes once we make it our concern to know God's will. Redirection sometimes arises out of a dissatisfaction with our present walk with the Lord or from a desire to know Him better. Guidance begins to reveal itself as we move on forward, exploring the options, rather than sitting and waiting. It is then, in this open attitude, that God frequently talks to us:

"Whether you turn to the right or to the left, your ears will hear a voice behind you, saying, 'This is the way, walk in it.'" (Isaiah 30:21)

Alexandra pointed out to me that you have to be moving forward along the way, in order to hear a voice coming from behind.

When we yielded to God, and arrived in the Philippines, I was reminded early on of God's love for the Filipino, a love that I too needed to emulate. On the front of the Filipino 500 peso banknote is inscribed: "The Filipino is worth dying for".

Most of our companions at language school had either come with a specific calling to a type of work or place, or since arriving in the Philippines, had felt comfortable serving within the Luktanon churches. We had not known any such comfort and were wondering why God had called us to serve in a land that already had growing churches and some able leaders and teachers? Filipinos seemed to be making a much better job of evangelising than ever we could with our fumbling Tagalog, and our not-so-smiley faces. But still, we accepted that we are not always given to understand our Father's plans from the outset and so we adopted the attitude to serve, to learn and to wait. How we needed first to give up our own prejudices, to lay aside our own preferences in order to receive a divine love for our fellow men.

Another two and quarter years passed from that first calling, before we eventually arrived among the Buhid. Only after three and a half years of language and cultural studies, and an apprenticeship under a Filipino pastor down in lowland Mindoro, were we able to move to the Buhid.

CHAPTER THREE

BUHID BEGINNINGS

"Miss Barham had a dog that she took with her wherever she went. Where Miss Barham went, there too the dog would follow. If she was talking to us for some time and the dog had wandered off somewhere, Miss Barham would whistle." Gaynop paused in his account to imitate the whistle before breaking off into an incredulous laugh. "And there and then the dog would appear!" he exclaimed with his brows raised in surprise.

There are several notable things about this information. Miss Barham was the first missionary to come to the Buhid, the first foreigner that many of them had ever seen and she obviously had made a vivid impression during her five-year stay among them. When Miss Barham came to the Buhid in 1952, after 23 years of working in China, Gaynop was not even born! But Gaynop could imitate the whistle as though he had been there himself. Buhid are fond of handing down stories as they pass the evenings around a smokey lamp. The story appealed to them because Buhid do not train their dogs to become companions and respond so promptly to a whistle.

The Buhid had been resistant to the gospel. They are by nature, suspicious of outsiders, and with good reason too, for they lost much land to Luktanon. The Luktanon had driven the non-confrontational Buhid and other Mangyan tribes off their ancestral lands, with beatings and threats, stealth, deceit and even murder.

The Buhid had a worldview which held that all people were contained within an enclosure and only the Buhid were free outside. Those within were sinners, murderers, cheats and such like. The Buhid were different, they were without sin, for they did not murder nor did they steal. They did not wear trousers because these were what sinners wore, nor would they use nails in building their homes for the same reason, but instead used vines to secure the bamboo slats to the floor joists and any other fixtures for which nails would usually be used. Many other such beliefs make them distinct and defiantly separate from those sinners within the enclosure.

Their forefathers also had prophecies, warning of strangers coming with a new teaching to lead them away from their beliefs. They were not to trust such teachers, as they would lead the Buhid into the enclosure to be ensnared.

The Tawbuid and Tadyawan, Mangyan tribes just to the north of the Buhid, had been positively prepared generations before for the coming of God's messengers, through a spirit, or dreams, speaking of a people very different from them, with white skin, who would bring a message that would liberate them from their fears. They would know who the true ones were because they would explain the good news in their tribal tongues.

Marie Barham experienced little encouragement in the Buhid's attitude towards the gospel. The Buhid grew accustomed to her visits, tolerated her and taught her their language, even providing suitable phrases for the gospel message to be explained in Buhid. But the Buhid carried on insisting that they had no sin, and would literally turn their backs on her when she tried to share Christ, muttering: "We do not know this Jesus, we don't understand your talk about him!"

Marie's praying began to take a new form: "Lord, if you want a corn of wheat to fall into the ground and die, let me be that one. I'm willing!"

Jesus teaches in John 12:24 that for as long as a grain of wheat remains a single seed, it cannot multiply. First it has to die, be buried in the ground, for new life to come, to produce many seeds. Jesus was referring to the necessity of His atoning death for man to be saved from the grip of sin and darkness, that through the death of Christ, all who put their faith in Him would be born into new and eternal life.

Christ goes on to teach about the meaning of discipleship, that we are not to live and hold on to this life only, but rather to consider it of far less value compared with eternal life. Christ calls us to follow Him, to abandon caution in this world and be committed to serving Him in the building of the Kingdom of God, even if that entails the laying down of our own lives. Our dying for the sake of Christ will not be to no avail, for God will honour such sacrifice.

Although turning 50, Marie was sprightly and could still hike the mountains of Mindoro with their deep mud, crossing rivers with waters up to chest height, and enduring leeches, snakes and tropical heat. Marie was strong and sturdy, able to suffer such conditions better than many men. However, Marie's new co-workers, Bob and Joy Hanselman, began to notice a change in her strength. Marie was supposed to have a medical check but had deferred the appointment more than once. Eventually she relented, went to Manila and was opened up, only for the surgeon to discover cancer rampant through her lungs. She wept on hearing the news, not so much for herself, but for the Buhid who still remained indifferent to the gospel.

During the time of hospital confinement in Manila, Marie

received a bag full of bamboo sections inscribed with Buhid ancient script scratched through the green membrane of the bamboo. These were "letters" from Buhid, written by using a stylus made from a small bamboo stem sharpened to a point, or by a small knife. They were reminding her that they were "praying" for her. She remembered her prayer based on John 12:24, and felt a peace mingled with a sense of destiny. She encouraged prayer supporters to keep on interceding for the Buhid, declaring: "I believe my death will turn out for their good!"

Back in her Canadian homeland, the doctors gave her two months to live. God gave her a remission, providing six months in which time Marie was able to prepare some gospel recordings. These were sent back to Mindoro for her co-workers to play to the Buhid. The Buhid were amazed at this talking box. When the handle was cranked, words came out, words in their language! They were more amazed that their friend, Miss Barham, could still speak to them from across the great ocean. She could still speak their language!

Marie's last letter to the Buhid was much prayed over. It reminded them of their tribal custom to grant the final wish of a dying person. She wished that those who had helped translate the gospel message into Buhid, "would truly repent and believe on the Lord Jesus". She concluded with the hope that she would be waiting to see many of them in heaven.

The OMF magazine, *Millions*, commented that Marie's dedication and self-sacrifice were not conditioned by success, but were offered to the Lord whose command was to "go into all the world". An obituary concluded with this challenge to the Church:

"Will you take on the burden of praying for the Buhid, that Marie's life's work may be perfected by a great turning to the Lord among the Buhid for whom Marie gladly fell into the ground and died?" (East Asia Millions, vol. 66, No. 7, N. American edition)

That challenge was taken up through the prayers of many around the world, together with workers committed to a self-sacrifice, similar to Marie's, for the task of evangelising. As the Lord called home the harbinger of His Good News, He did not leave himself without a witness, for the Hanselmans became spiritual parents to many Buhid, giving an entire working lifetime to explain the gospel and ground in the truth those who were being saved.

Their work had many strands. God's word needed to be written down for the young church to really become established in the truth. This presented the problem of what script to use, for the Buhid script, considered to be of Indic origin, differed markedly between the north and south of the Buhid area, so that no single script was mutually intelligible. The Latin script, introduced by the Spanish and used by all main Filipino languages, was adopted for the Buhid, a significant step in assisting their future integration into Filipino society. Using this script, literacy programmes were run in every village that had responded to Christ. The Hanselmans also prepared many Bible study materials pitched at the appropriate level, taking into account their cultural and pagan background, for the materials used in the Luktanon churches with their Roman Catholic background and Spanish/American culture were quite often unsuitable.

Other responsibilities were added to the Hanselmans' emerging role, such as attending to health needs since there were no medical facilities in the tribal area or even close by. Medical treatment in the towns was fraught with all the attendant difficulties that a marginalised people encounter, despised and derided by the supercilious Luktanon. The missionaries became bridge builders between tribe and town, to inspire sympathy, understanding and trust, facilitating relationships between the two. A livelihood project was also set up to help the poorer families to earn some cash.

Their last work was the major task of translating the New Testament into Buhid. This translation was dedicated in 1988 when they retired from the work. The Hanselmans left the four main churches under trained leaders, equipped not only with God's word, but with volumes of Bible studies and notes, a hymnal incorporating notes on how to conduct anything from baptismal classes to funerals. It would have appeared to many that the work had been completed very thoroughly: no further full-time missionaries would be needed.

In 1994 the Hanselmans made a last visit to the Buhid from their retirement in the States, to correct the Buhid translation of the Chronological Bible course. By then it was becoming clear that we were to be assigned initially to the Buhid, to gain some understanding of tribal culture before becoming itinerant amongst other tribes to undertake leadership training. The Hanselmans invited us to come over from Batangas (where we were still studying Tagalog, in an interminable fashion, at the language school), to meet them in their rented home down in the lowland town of Bongabong before travelling together to Batangan, one of the main Buhid villages with a church.

The road to Batangan from Bongabong followed low, rolling ridge tops, drawing us closer to the central mountain chain. The journey came to a halt at the broad Bongabong River. The jeepney (an elongated US army jeep), was unable to cross the river as the bridge had been washed away in the floods of 1993, and the local municipality, not having sufficient funds, had been unable to rebuild it.

Everyone clambered down the bank to the river's flood plain. Thankfully the river was low, confined to just one main channel at the far side of the valley. Across this stony wilderness, over the uneven boulders, we walked with some difficulty, with our baggage and our children. We reached a footbridge made from sections of bamboo and some straightish tree limbs, fastened in a higgledy-piggledy fashion by nail and rope. It looked most suspect with its narrow, crooked course of gangplanks, spanning a fast-flowing river. The bridge, clearly a local effort, appeared to have evolved rather than been constructed to any plan. One could almost picture a crew of beer-swilling locals from the village of Lisap, just on the far side, putting this bridge up after one of their drinking sprees. But it served its purpose admirably and brought a certain revenue to the town by way of a toll collected by some unfriendly youths.

Here at this bridge we first became aware of another companion in our party, a 20-year-old Buhid by the name of Moses. He picked up little Hannah in one arm as she hesitated about stepping onto this structure, and carried her swiftly over to the far side. We enjoyed to the full the revelation that his name was Moses, the one to lead us across the waters!

Lisap is a lawless place, at one time a favoured ambush locality for the NPA (the Communist New People's Army), ideal for that purpose with its rocky escarpment, thick with bush scrub, which came right up to the bridge end at the start of the village. A surprise attack on police vehicles, or a hold-up on jeepney or bus, was easily executed in such a location.

Lisap was also a lowland frontier town, the nearest road point to a trans-island trail, the gathering place of many Buhid farmers who sold their bananas on Saturdays to the traders who came here from Roxas and Bongabong and beyond. There was something of a fairground feel to the place on those market days, with the garishly painted stalls set up for gambling games, attracting many tribesfolk to risk a peso or two. The wayside was decorated with a vast array of plastic wares, buckets and laundry basins all in glossy, primary colours. There was even a cinema! Once I gained permission to sneak a peak inside. Cinema was a grandiose name for a not-so-very-large room inside a tin shack, furnished with rows of wooden benches all facing a television screen and video recorder, powered by a diesel generator. But this was a great novelty to many who had never been to a real cinema, nor had often seen a television.

The Roxas jeepney took us along the road on the far side of the broken bridge. After only five minutes, we were disembarking again, beginning the 40-minute or so trek up the Batangan River valley to the Buhid settlement of that name. "Batangan of the Interior" as some referred to it, suggested a place of detachment from all that was familiar, a village tucked away, concealed in the folds of the rising mountains. The walk was delightful, once the shade of the jungle and hillside was reached. But first the fierce heat bearing down from a cloudless sky and the glare reflecting up from the white rock strewn profusely along the valley floor had to be endured. The river made a natural clearing through the semi-cultivated jungle, and the trail followed its banks. Here, many varieties of fruit-bearing trees replaced the former rainforest. It still felt wild, though, for the imported trees were not set in rows, nor even in groups of lime and mandarin orange trees, coconut palms and soursop, but instead were planted to provide an assortment of fruit to the self-sufficient farmer who did not have extensive land.

We slaked our thirst with spring water conveyed along a long, split bamboo section, before coming onto the Buhid village itself. The main street stood immediately before us, even boasting a concreted section. The appearance of such a street was totally unexpected and struck us as an anomaly, standing in isolation, not joined to anything that could really pass for a road. Lining the main street were the stalls and eating-houses run by the Luktanon. It had something of the hard feel of Lisap about it, with its busy commerce, but the difference was the number of Buhid about, who far outnumbered the Luktanon. It was a less threatening place than Lisap, there being no drunks to noisily greet and latch onto the foreigner, no one who jauntily walked about the place showing they belonged and that this was their town. The Buhid were discreet, even as a crowd. They flashed shy smiles at us and looked away before taking a longer, furtive scrutiny when we were not facing in their direction. They walked quietly, almost apologetically, without any apparent purpose in mind, but with an aim that only they knew, concealed from the onlooker.

The contrast was startling. Even when they dress themselves up, groom their appearance identically to the Luktanon and wear the latest fashion in haircut, the Mangyan stand out prominently from the Luktanon, because of their walk and whole gentle manner. Even the occasional dog owned by the Mangyan walks and behaves in a Mangyan way, whereas the dogs of the Luktanon are aggressive, trained by being teased and taunted, tied up for the purpose of becoming guard dogs.

The Hanselmans were extremely gracious with us on that first and only night in Batangan. Ligaya (Joy) had polished the wooden floorboards in our honour with half of a very thick and fibrous coconut shell. They gave up the one bed in the house for us, insisting that they would be quite comfortable sleeping on the floor beside the kitchen table. The afternoon of our arrival, we sat with Bob underneath an immense mango tree beside our neighbour's house and became acquainted a little with the Buhid, who thankfully could speak Tagalog, many of them better than we could. A couple in their thirties came to the house early evening to check translation work that Joy had done. Meanwhile Bob cooked supper on a paraffin stove. After supper, one or two church elders came along.

"Visitors from the hills have just arrived!" they announced, a euphemism informing us that the NPA were in the village. The Hanselmans made the decision to leave at first light rather than stay around for the Sunday worship service.

So our first trip to Batangan came to an abrupt end, a total of about fifteen hours in duration. The visit and the Hanselmans made a strong impression upon us, one that was to remain and motivate us through the remainder of language school and the almost two years that followed whilst serving our apprenticeship under a Tagalog pastor in Victoria – a lowland, Mindoro town.

CHAPTER FOUR

THE MAN SAVED BY A SNEEZE

The tropical night seemed endless with its electrifying buzz of cicadas and other insects making unbelievably loud sawing and whirring noises through the night. The moon had eased its way through the treetops of the hills round about, and now shone upon the large leathery leaves of the kamansi tree. Far away, many, many miles distant, beyond the very shores of Mindoro, the thunder rolled and faint flashes of lightning troubled the horizon. It was a long night, especially for the one who gave birth to a boy, a healthy lad who cried with determination as he came into that dark and troubled world.

The parents were not pleased.

They already had three sons, all close in age and still none of them big enough to be of much help in the fields. All through the pregnancy, they had wondered how they were to provide for yet another mouth to feed, another body to look after.

The mother placed the boy on a rush mat and, taking a strip of rattan, she gathered up the two long sides of the mat and began to sew by passing the sharpened end of rattan through between the mat's sides. She busied herself in this manner whilst her husband was away digging a hole some distance away from their home. It was quicker digging at this hour, for the air was cool and fresh in the hills at night. In the daytime, it would have taken twice as long. Besides he wanted to get the grim task over and done with.

"It's ready," the man announced a while later to his wife, as he quietly slipped into the house beside her. The mother had nearly finished her work of preparing the coffin, only about six inches remained to be stitched up. The father stooped over the nearly sewn-up mat and looked in through the remaining gap. He could just see his son's head. At that moment the baby sneezed, a pagan sign to his parents that the spirit had entered the child. It was taboo to bury a baby alive once his spirit had come.

A meaningful glance was exchanged between the couple, the wife suddenly ceasing her activity.

The baby survived the first six months of life and was given the name Monay. Children among the Buhid are not named early on, due to the high mortality rate. The giving of a name signifies the first triumph in a person's life, the triumph of living through those delicate months when perhaps as many as 25 to 30 percent die in infancy. Buhid names rarely have any meaning and this was so in Monay's case.

Monay was in his early teens when he really began to understand the Bible message taught by the Hanselmans. On becoming a believer, Monay recognised God had intervened in that first hour of his birth by making him sneeze.

Out of gratitude and a growing relationship with God, Monay decided to dedicate his life to serving Christ. The Hanselmans encouraged him to go to the Mangyan Bible School at the foot of Mt. Halcon. He graduated some three years later.

Monay joined a team of Buhid missionaries, across the central mountain chain, over on the western side of Mindoro, reaching Buhid people there with the gospel in a place called Datag Bonglay. The Buhid were accompanied by an Australian couple, Bill and Marlene Doust. The people there were resistant, and the situation was further complicated by a long-standing feud between the two clans who lived in the area.

Waydinan and his wife were the older of the several Buhid missionaries. It was this same Waydinan who later had had that burden to pray for a missionary family five years after the Hanselman's retirement, during that September of 1993, the prayer that had been answered by the Lord calling us.

One day, a drunken Luktanon picked a meaningless quarrel with Waydinan. Waydinan was an obedient man of God whose fearless attitude, before the verbal aggression of this drunkard, incensed the Luktanon so much that he struck Waydinan in the face.

Recalling the scripture, Waydinan offered his other cheek, perhaps rather hoping that by obeying a command of the Lord, he would be delivered from this dangerous situation.

Waydinan was struck again with such force that he was felled to the ground and then kicked in the face. His companions led him back east along the long, trans-island trek to consult the Hanselmans at Batangan. Waydinan's face became badly swollen with infection as well as bruising. He was taken to a clinic in the lowlands where the wounds had to be lanced. The doctor remarked that many facial bones had been broken. Where had God been?

Not long after this incident, the Luktanon fell into a fight with someone else, who, showing no such restraint, pulled a knife on him, ending his life. Maybe he had received his just deserts?

The church planting at Datag Bonglay continued. A core of people became committed to meeting and worshipping the Lord, trusting Him when a family member became sick, instead of chanting to the spirits of the dead. The work did come to an end, for it seemed to have found its growth limit, greatly impaired by the clan feud. The missionaries went home, east over the mountains, leaving behind a few able to lead meetings and share something from God's word. But the general feeling had been one of defeat, for few had accepted the Lord.

Monay returned to serve the Batangan church. Not all was well here either. The numbers attending the Sunday morning worship services might have looked encouraging, but for many churchgoers that was the sum total of their spiritual lives: a three-hour appearance a week to placate the Lord so that His wrath would not be incurred! Hopefully, many reasoned, they might prosper because of their show of worship.

Their mindset was still pagan. Worshipping in the house of the Lord became a substitute for the offering of food placed outside the house to placate the ancestral spirits. Although Buhid understood God to be more powerful and more benevolent than the demon spirits, there lingered their centuries-old fear of the spirits to whom they had to pay homage. They naturally brought these attitudes with them into their Christian lives. They could relate to God as the Father, but a stern father who needed a show of respect and obedience to appease his displeasure with them; a model drawn as much from their own father/child relationships, and based on the obligation upon the living to serve the needs of their dead ancestors.

When the church elders encouraged others to be more faithful to the Lord, they most often chastised the lukewarm Christians with threats of God's judgement that would befall them in this life as well as on the great judgement day of God, should they not turn from their evil ways. Any misfortune that occurred was often explained by the more zealous as an instance of God showing his displeasure with a half-hearted individual. Sometimes they were right to point this out, when the misfortune was in direct consequence of a sin committed, for example, when Cain was made a fugitive after murdering Abel. But such continual bias about judgement, to the exclusion of a God who forgives and gives the repentant a new start, does not encourage love for God, nor does it stir up a willingness to serve Him out of gratitude. It results in a warped view of God as the tyrant who can cause you to become sick: all sickness therefore is due to sin! The Buhid believers lacked natural passion for the Lord and consequently were more concerned with performing the absolute minimum to secure their position of favour, making a religion out of their doing, rather than worshipping in response to a relationship with God, initiated through God's love for us, and demonstrated so powerfully through the cross.

There were of course exceptions to this spiritual indifference. Monay was a case in point, and others too, who had grasped the fuller revelation of God. But even men like Monay, despite knowing the pardon and love of the Lord, still were uncertain about how to communicate this.

The Western Church today so often steers clear from mentioning judgement that the non-Christian asks: what is Christ saving man from? If we ignore the certainty of judgement, we lose something of the urgent desire to save the non-Christian from the horrors that Christ went to some length to illustrate. God's wrath is righteous, reasonable, justified because He judges justly, for He sees the whole picture, even the hidden motives of man's heart. Judgement reminds us of our accountability, the importance of keeping a short account with God, not to mention the need for personal holiness.

There is something absolutely appealing in God's holiness, greatly adding to our ability to adore the Lord. Perhaps a heightened awareness of the beauty of holiness is gained after having lived in a place where corruption and embezzlement are the norm? Dwelling on the wrath of God helps us to appreciate even more His mercy and love for us who certainly have not earned such forgiveness.

It is essential to maintain a balance between God's holiness and God's love for all people. Ignore the one and emphasise the other and we have a lop-sided gospel, an incorrect understanding of the person of God and an incomplete knowledge of how we ought to respond to Him. When the emphasis is on the love of God, we lose something of the awe and majesty, the holy fear and reverence of the Lord. Ignore the love of God and the Church responds out of a sense of duty, not out of adoration.

* * *

We made our base in Batangan for the six remaining months of our first missionary term (four years). Ernesto was the one who brought us and our belongings to this easily accessible village, in the mission four-wheel-drive vehicle able to ford the river crossings. That first evening, the church elders and many more besides, met in the front room of our tribal house. In reply to Ernesto's question as to what their expectations of us were, the Buhid replied that they wanted "to grow in Christ". One added that he would like some help in teaching the youth in the village. This was an auspicious start.

Being in leadership is often lonely, especially if there are no other like-minded individuals to whom you can really unburden your heart. It soon became clear that this was a much-needed role, providing the opportunity for such men who labour, often quite fruitlessly, in isolated places, to have the right to be heard and the comfort of being prayed for. Sometimes we could point them to a scripture that would provide the guidance they needed, or an answer to a problem that had perplexed. At other times, owing to our own ignorance, or sometimes the silence of scripture, we could not immediately provide the counsel they requested, but even then, there was still the encouragement of being understood, of not feeling all alone, out on a limb. Sometimes after praying and further meditation over a problem, light would be given by the Lord to help us see the issue through His perspective and so overcome what was no longer just their problem, but rather our joint obstacle. The leaders felt often misunderstood, men in whom the churches had unrealistic expectations in terms of biblical knowledge and Christian duty.

We began our ministry in Batangan with daily Bible studies I had prepared a year before, whilst still serving my apprenticeship.

These materials had served the purpose of completing part of the requirement of the language school. However I had hoped that the compilation of these notes, entitled "Keys to Victorious Christian Living", would meet more than just an academic need, but when they failed to arouse interest, I had been disappointed. On hearing the Batangan elders' request, their desire to grow in Christ, the Keys to Victorious Christian Living course suddenly came to mind. I realised that the Lord had me prepare in advance for this moment, suitable materials that could be used immediately. It was significant too that the course took six months to complete, the last lesson being taught on more or less the last day before we left Batangan for our first home assignment!

These Bible studies convened at six in the morning outside our home, with benches drawn up around a fire. We wanted to make it accessible to all and wrongly thought that the church building might put some off attending. It was heart-warming to see the Buhid appear in ones and twos out of the semi-gloom before the sun had risen over the brow of the hill. They emerged all of a sudden, their approach silent as they mostly went barefoot. If they wore flip-flops, they didn't shuffle them along the ground in the manner of the Luktanon, but still walked furtively, as though they were stalking some bird. Attendance was initially very good, but soon diminished as our novelty value faded. But we did not lose heart, for there was a faithful core who really began to participate and air their concerns and objections.

Monay was the one who most frequently stopped me in my teaching, seeking clarification. Sometimes I assumed too much knowledge. At other times my examples were not at all suited to an Iron Age, tribal culture, such as when I compared the need for reliance on the Holy Spirit to an engine's need for oil. Other times it was my own inexperience, of inadequately explaining the scriptures or providing inadequate application. I had not been a Bible teacher, or a preacher, back in Scotland, having only used Bible study materials prepared by others for Sunday school classes. But sometimes Monay objected to what I said as being different from his own experience. This was not done in any contrary way, with a partisan-like attitude; that is not the way of Orientals. These questions and objections were the genuine heart-searchings of a man desperate to know God better.

Monay was troubled by the seeming defeat of the mission to Datag Bonglay. He was concerned, for example, with why Waydinan was hit on the other cheek when he offered it to his adversary? Had they not left fields, families and homes, just as the Bible instructs in Mark 10:29, to bring the Good News to the other side of the island? Had God not promised to be with those who went to make disciples (Matt. 28:18–20)? So why the setbacks and the persecutions and the lack of growth in that church, especially when the workers were plentiful in this instance? Not all his questions could be answered, but at least some could be from scripture. The Hanselmans had trained them well to expect a teacher to answer their questions by opening God's word to them. They were not so interested in one's own opinions, or secular theories, such was their high regard of scripture that I have not encountered to such a degree in the West, with the promulgation of so much teaching borrowed from many disciplines other than God's word. The correct starting ground has always to be scripture, which later can be supported or added to, with appeal to another discipline.

Seeing Monay, others and ourselves progress in our understanding of God was a great joy – as we searched the scriptures as to why Christians encountered persecution. Here again, God had already prepared me for thinking biblically through this very issue! When I was at Bible college, I wrote an exegesis of New Testament texts on my own chosen theme of "God's Purposes in a Believer's Sufferings". It is marvellous to look back on God prompting us to prepare something which doesn't have an immediate application to a work we are presently engaged in, but one for which we feel strangely motivated to pursue and to prepare. Such instances make us realise, with wonder, the many strands that make up our calling, in fulfilling God's purposes.

Jesus had warned his disciples that just as He was persecuted, so would we be (John 15:20), the experience often of those who declared the gospel throughout the account in the book of Acts. Suffering for doing what is right, one of the themes of Peter's first letter, is not something that should surprise us, since it is the authentic mark of discipleship. The powers and authorities in this world will oppose the Christian message, since the gospel challenges the old order and the former lords who will not yield without a fight.

I like to attribute the small breakthrough in the church at Datag Bonglay, following soon after the incident when Waydinan was beaten up, to the fact he had turned the other cheek. By this he had demonstrated fearlessness in the face of violence, trusting in His Lord to work it out for the good of the Kingdom. It might not have turned out in quite the way Waydinan and the other missionaries had anticipated, but pagans had witnessed his stand and perhaps had pondered the motivation of this man, who believed in what he taught, to love even your enemies and to leave vengeance to the Lord. God moves in unexpected ways. The more I reflect on what happened, the more I believe God used the incident for the good of His Church, drawing others to Himself. Certainly when the Jerusalem church was being arrested and in some instances executed by Saul and other Pharisees, the gospel spread and took root. God does draw good out of persecution. The powers of darkness may appear to triumph, to gain the upper hand for a time, but God will honour the sacrifices made by His people who have acted in faith.

As our first term drew to a speedy and satisfying close, we began already to look ahead to our second term and its goals. The Buhid church elders had discussed our return and found one in their number able to write quaintly, in high-school English, a request to the "Church in Scotland" asking for the return of their missionaries for the purpose of evangelism and teaching. The Buhid were wonderfully naïve about denominations. It had not occurred to them to address this letter to anyone, other than to the Church in Scotland and they were quite correct in addressing it as such. OMF, being both a facilitator to individual churches, as well as drawing members from a wide range of denominations, did indeed represent an aspect of the Church in Scotland. Those who prayed and supported us were from this nationwide assortment of churches in that land and beyond.

We made visits to the other Buhid churches, to see their situations and to listen to the concerns of their leaders before going on home assignment. We observed the signs of nominalism, folk ignoring the sermon, talking quite unperturbedly in the pews, drowning the embarrassed voice of the preacher, even cracking jokes and laughing instead of singing worship to the Lord, and deliberately breaking wind to bring down howls of laughter when someone was praying or giving a report from the front. Many had no respect for, or love of, God's word. One old fellow would always make a point of stretching himself out full length on the pew whenever I got up to preach and would soon be peacefully asleep, giving little encouragement to someone who had, up until that time, done very little preaching in English let alone another language.

Besides the apparent need to bring many of the young couples to Christ and truly ground the Buhid in the scriptures, it was apparent that the gospel had only reached the periphery of the tribal area, with large areas still without a witness and a whole sub-tribe – the Bangon – without a Christian. This was the big challenge facing the Buhid: to resurrect the vision for outreach and push the Kingdom frontiers forward, higher up into the hills to a people waiting in darkness, plagued by fears, ensnared by taboos, living under the rule of the demonic prince.

The situation challenged us and we were glad to have the opportunity to return to the Church in Scotland, to share the burden God had lain on our hearts, to describe the situation and to enlist their prayer support. For this purpose many missionaries return home. Without that concentration of prayer, what could we, a missionary family, hope to achieve?

J.O. Fraser, the missionary to the Lisu tribe of China, had taught about the necessity for prayer for breakthrough in frontline places. He likened the work of a missionary to a man who tried to push a boat off a sandbank into the water all on his own. As hard as he tried, the heavy boat would not shift. But when he prayed and called on others to pray for a specific situation, and waited for the help of the Lord, the accumulative effect of believing prayer was like the rising tide, easily lifting and freeing that boat once stuck fast in the mud. Before he appealed for the prayers of supporters back on the homeside, the work was making very little progress, or at best every progress was marked by a setback, as Lisu came to faith then slid back into their old ways again. Once Fraser began sending updates on the progress of the work to those who had covenanted their daily prayer support, listing needs for prayer, God began to bless the work in a way Fraser had never seen before. Lisu began to stand steadfast in Christ in spite of trials and temptations.

We sensed our return to the Buhid would be challenged by the powers of darkness once we called people to repentance. We expected the anger of the shamen when folk turned away from them to follow God. This was enemy territory, and these were strongholds held for centuries by Satan who was not going to relinquish his grip overnight. Yet we had the confidence of victory, certainly not in anything that we had to offer, but in the victory that Christ has already won, the release from the old order of fear. Christ made the same proclamation when he began His public ministry at the synagogue in Nazareth:

"The Spirit of the Lord is on me, because he has anointed me to preach good news to the poor. He has sent me to proclaim freedom for the prisoners and recovery of sight for the blind, to release the oppressed, to proclaim the year of the Lord's favour." (Luke 4:18–19)

* * *

Like many missionaries, we had some major issues to work through during our home assignment, threatening the possibility of our return. Hannah had started to hyper-ventilate halfway through the furlough period and many came to the immediate conclusion that she was dreading going back to Asia, fearing the separation from us at boarding school.

But we saw things differently. My mother had died just a few weeks before these panic attacks and Hannah was grieving for a dearly-loved granny whom she had only really come to know a few months earlier. They shared the same passion for painting and had many other interests in common. Hannah was diagnosed as struggling with a loss factor which induced these hyper-ventilation attacks. Besides the significant loss of a beloved granny, there was the loss too of all that was familiar: Asian culture, Chefoo School, special school friends, as well as friends within the OMF family, to name but a few.

Home assignment was not all what we had expected either, bringing a certain amount of disillusionment. I spent frequent periods away from home, talking to different churches and groups, mostly around Scotland but also down in England, contrary to our hopes of having at least a year of being together. Sometimes we all needed to attend a meeting, and it caused real tension as we felt that we had become public property. No single stress caused Hannah's condition, but all these factors taken together resulted in a high accumulation of stress bringing about the attacks.

It was difficult to go back while wrestling with these stresses. We listened to much well-meant advice, that our first duty was to our children and therefore we had the obligation to stay at home. But as the weeks passed and the time approached when the mission and we ourselves had to make a decision about returning, Hannah's panic attacks lessened in frequency, but did not disappear altogether. We were taught how to help Hannah's condition as well as praying ardently for her healing but we had no guarantee that these attacks would cease once we returned to Asia. These were dark times of doubt and soul-searching, trying to balance a clear calling to return to the Buhid, with a loving, responsible attitude towards our children, and in holding these two together, exercising the faith that God knows and cares and can carry us through.

I went for a long hike in the Scottish hills one day, casting all these anxieties on the Lord and came back home a renewed man. I had met with the Lord, for He had heard my cry and given me the confidence to leave these concerns with Him for He cares and He would work it out for us. It boiled down to a matter of trust. I had spent the day talking to the Lord and in return He gave me a peace and confidence that I could rely on Him. I firmly believe that if God calls, He will also enable, whatever the obstacles, faith overcoming the despair of faithless reflection.

CHAPTER FIVE

CONTESTED CLAIM

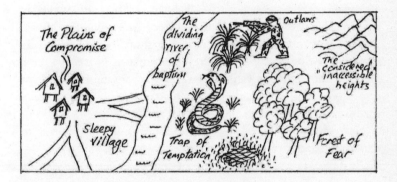

We woke together in the middle of the night, both of us in a cold sweat. Someone was stalking around just outside our hut in Siyangi. Across the field, the elderly shaman was still singing to the spirits of the dead. He had been chanting when we settled down to sleep after ten o'clock and now in the middle of the night, he was still monotonously droning out the repetitious request, but now with greater fervour and joined by another. We assumed someone in the village was sick and had asked for his intercession.

We were told never to open the door to anyone at such a time of night, as bandits and soldiers of the NPA made a habit of calling on folk at such an hour. No sooner had you opened the door than you were either knocked over the head and had your possessions worked over or were threatened at gunpoint and instructed to hand over any money and valuables. In our case, since we were deemed to be rich foreigners, or employees of an organisation that would supposedly pay out any sum demanded, there was the added risk of being kidnapped and held hostage for a ransom.

Lying on bamboo slats tied to floor beams, we felt hands busy tying something to the joists and could hear the breath of the individual just on the other side of the woven bamboo partition that was our outside wall. The pervasive evil made us want to do something quickly before being paralysed by fear.

"O Lord, rescue us from those who mean to do us harm . . ." We managed to stammer out aloud as we began to pray, helpless a moment before in the evil clutches, helpless that was until we began to pray. Then we could remind ourselves of God's almighty power, and the believer's ability to stand in Christ and counter whatever curse was being put upon us. Prayer brought us peace, the tying stopped and someone walked away. After thanking the Lord for His protection, we wonderfully managed to get back to sleep again.

Next morning, we asked our neighbour, a fellow believer, to explain the significance of the previous night.

He replied with a laugh: a curse of death had been placed upon us!

Without the knowledge that Christ was with us, and far greater than all the power of the demons combined, we would have been most uneasy, and perhaps even would have started to panic. We had little experience of the occult first-hand before coming to the Philippines. But we knew prayer could break such evil power. We prayed there and then with the neighbour, who by this time had been joined by his son-in-law, that these curses would be rendered ineffective.

"They will not expect you to live past noon," the older one pointed out. I smiled. I was not sure whether he was trying to humour us, or whether he perhaps believed that we would die by the morning's end. I reiterated my confidence that our Lord is almighty and that, God willing, He would not yet allow His servants to perish at the commencement of our second term and give the appearance that the old lords were greater than the Lord of whom we preached.

The Siyangi church had invited us to come and teach, but not all in the village were Christian. Almost half were still pagan or had backslided into animistic ways once again. The shaman did not appreciate our being there, since our presence apparently interfered with his powers.

When I came to read Psalm 91 some months after this incident, I was struck by how applicable these verses are to that encounter in the middle of the night. It opens with the well-known verse: "He who dwells in the shelter of the Most High will rest in the shadow of the Almighty."

I thought back to that oppressive moment when someone was tying the curse to our house in the dead of night, and the conscious effort we had to make to pray, to dwell in God's presence. It had been like a trial of strength; a great effort had to be summoned to resist the urge to give in. Once we put up our shield of faith and struck back with the sword of the Spirit, then the peace came, a calm that remained even after learning of the evil intent of the shamen and his cronies. God promises to those who abide in Him, the resting in His shadow, the protection of His wings over and about us.

"You will not fear the terror of the night," the psalmist wrote in verse five, echoing our own experience of God's faithfulness as being our shield. It does not depend on our faithfulness, but on God's absolute trustworthiness. He alone is capable of sustaining us through the onslaughts of the enemy, provided we make the effort to approach his "dwelling" place and shelter under His wings.

The curse was of course broken. The very thing that Satan used to try to cast us out and cause fear through the Buhid believers, was the instrument that God used to demonstrate His unsurpassing power, that He is the Lord and able to sustain His servants.

This had been our first proper visit to Siyangi. From the washed-away road bridge where Moses had carried Hannah across on the makeshift footbridge, it was a two-hour walk up a shadeless flood plain to reach this Buhid village. The track had the habit of fading away in the vast sprawl of boulders, scattered by the last flood across the wide margins on either side of the river.

The Buhid sought us out with a childlike glee, so appreciative we had come to stay with them for a while. Grandparents came with gifts of sweet potato or a bunch of bananas and would pass the time of day reminiscing about Roberto and Ligaya. There was never a quiet moment, for no sooner had one lot of visitors left, than the next were there. Therefore it did not seem so onerous to meet their request of having three teaching sessions daily, each lasting up to two hours, the evening one lasting longer as they were loathe to break up the meetings.

The atmosphere in the church on the first teaching day was more akin to that of a pub than of a church. Extremely high-spirited, they had their fair share of pranksters. The back row had all the young men together, their wives sitting forward on the benches with their youngsters and babies at the breast. The young dads looked as though they were going to be hard work, there for a laugh at the expense of these funny-looking missionaries who spoke Tagalog and some Buhid in a most amusing way.

We had most inappropriately brought booklets in which they were to write their answers in the spaces provided under the questions. Most of them had not written for years, since they were at school, or had been taught by the Hanselmans. Holding a pencil or ball pen correctly in callused hands used to heavy work was a challenge in itself. Some were totally illiterate. But rather than being put off, many of them saw the writing as a challenge and the illiterate contented themselves with watching their companions in their unaccustomed toil. However, we did understandably lose one or two of the illiterate ones because of this.

The course encouraged them to share their understanding of the various Bible texts that outlined God's redemptive work for man. The literate ones were not at a stage to write in their independent answers. Rather we made each question a discussion topic in which they contributed their answers and then we composed an appropriate sentence or two on the blackboard as a summary which they duly copied down.

It took them quite a while to realise they needed to look for the answers in the Bible text and not just reply with their own interpretation, although the latter was most instructive for us to understand more of the Buhid mindset. This became good preparation for them to learn instinctively to dig into the Bible text and find the gems hidden there. As one of them put it, it was like digging in some promising-looking ground on the hillside looking for wild sweet potatoes. The presence of the sweet potato was not always immediately obvious, since it grew in places overgrown with weed. The first digging didn't always reveal the sweet potato, for sometimes you had to go deeper than expected and were often rewarded by a larger-than-usual potato.

This promised to be a steep learning curve for us as well, to communicate in a Buhid way and drop the many unintelligible analogies that are useful in a Western, high-tech society.

All dutifully copied down the summaries in their answer books. Alexandra and I did the rounds of the benches to encourage them on, pointing out when they had missed a whole line from the board. Much laughter and high jinks greeted us when we approached the back row. If it was Alexandra coming to check on them, one or two of them would mysteriously contract cramp in their hand. They never harassed her, but took every opportunity to lure Alexandra over for assistance. When I came to the rescue, their hand would recover all of a sudden or they could now see clearly the writing on the chalkboard. Young mothers had their hands full, trying to write on their lap or upon the bench to their side whilst breast-feeding. The babies were often troublesome, recognising that they were not getting the full attention they were accustomed to and would protest by giving up on the breast offered to them. Some simply needed winding. But it was a credit to all of them for persevering. We apologised for doing something which perhaps after all was not very appropriate.

"No – this is good for us," returned the young couples. "We have not written for ages and haven't had the Bible opened up in this manner before!"

By day three, we noticed a change had come over the congregation, which still to our surprise was meeting in large numbers. The young fathers were still there on the back row, but they were no longer rowdy, but quiet, studious, keen to ask questions to understand a spiritual point, for now they were anxious to learn God's plan of salvation for them. As we walked around, we heard comments being made to the one sitting beside them: "I'm finished with sin. From now on I'm going to follow the Lord!"

Those were heady days, days that significantly marked a new beginning particularly with the young couples that made up well over half of the church. Such intensive days left us exhausted and often really struggling at bedtime just to convert our tiny one-room house from the daytime use of dining area/study into the nighttime purpose of a bedroom. When we lay down lengthways inside the house, my feet were touching the far wall whilst my head touched the near wall.

That first trip into Siyangi was the nine-day trip we made during this new missionary term, three months on from discovering I had contracted TB. It had been a shock to be informed by a German doctor that a tuberculosis cloud in my upper left lung was apparent on the x-ray. I had been carrying it, by his reckoning, for eighteen months – it had been contracted at the end of our first term – which explained why my energy level had dropped even in the cool climate of Scotland, when you would have expected the reverse, and why I was getting a mild sweat at night! I was no longer able to climb as many of the Scottish hills, known as munroes, in a day as I had been able to four years previously. I put it down to getting into my forties! I reflected that I was not like my father who found his stamina had reached a peak in his early forties. The medication made me feel much worse. It seemed to sap what energy I had and made me feel nauseous. Often I would get a sudden sinking feeling as though I were fading away. But I did not lose consciousness during that period.

Instead of being able to head straight back into the tribal villages immediately on our return from Scotland, I was sent to convalesce at the Calapan mission home. There I managed to prepare some sermons and Bible study materials when strength permitted. However I had to be cautious, for I had much good advice from Anni, our deputy team leader who was also a nurse by training: I was to rest to allow a full recovery. This, taken together with the natural anxiety of a wife, thankfully limited what I could do.

God's ways are not our ways. I had to learn not to take good health for granted, however much I needed my strength to manage the climbing in the hot tropics. There is no guarantee that the servant of God is immune from the diseases that hit other people. It would be arrogant to expect special compensation as a missionary in the light of Christ's sufferings and Paul who endured all kinds of hardships (2 Corinthians 6:4–10 & 11:23–29).

During that convalescence, I received a letter from Iain McDonald, a Scottish minister friend, passing on the observation made by a fellow minister who was often frustrated by recurrent health problems necessitating enforced rest from the ministry. That minister was eventually able to rejoice in his infirmities as he recognised that God had laid him aside to draw him closer to Himself. He came to know the Father in a deeper and more intimate way than he ever could have done while dashing around with abounding health, attending to all the demands of the ministry. In the long run, the minister's congregation benefited from the rich insights into God's character that he had been able to glean because of those times of enforced rest! I treasured that gem of wisdom which further reconciled me with what had happened.

This led me deeper in my understanding of what Paul wrote in his second letter to the Corinthians:

"If I must boast, I will boast of the things that show my weakness."

It is a surprising statement to make to his accusers, who considered themselves more spiritual than Paul himself. Paul came to recognise that his worth lay not in his wide knowledge and great wisdom, but in his conviction that these things were worthless compared to the power of Christ within us. Not only can knowledge be worthless, but it can obstruct what Christ seeks to do in us and through us. Paul develops this whole idea in 2 Corinthians 12:8–10 with the statement:

"Three times I pleaded with the Lord to take it [*the thorn in his flesh*] away from me. But He said to me, 'My grace is sufficient for you, for my power is made perfect in weakness.' Therefore I will boast all the more gladly about my weaknesses, so that Christ's power may rest on me. That is why, for Christ's sake, I delight in weaknesses, in insults, in hardships, in persecutions, in difficulties. For when I am weak, then I am strong."

That first visit to Siyangi showed something of the blessing of the Lord through a weak and imperfect servant. The months leading up to that visit resulted in my becoming more intimate with the Lord. I was humbled in a way that taught me to rely more totally on Him. We went to Siyangi concerned as to how my strength would last and we were more prayerful because of this weakness, seeking God to bring blessing rather than automatically working ever harder at preparing materials and polishing the presentation. More time was given to prayer rather than to perfecting further our human effort. It is liberating to discover that we need to admit our own weakness, our own impotence, to bring God's blessing.

The battle for the souls of men and women in Siyangi was intense. The curse of death might have been rendered ineffective, but some curse appeared to remain upon me in particular. Now it is understandable that whilst still recovering from TB and being subjected to constant attention from the villagers (which reached an almost adulatory level on that first visit, thankfully diminishing on subsequent stays), that I was not able to remain the full nine days proposed for that visit. I had just reached exhaustion point. The contrast between what I experienced now, and the three months of quiet and solitude beforehand, was indeed great. But on subsequent visits we were never able to teach for the full nine days either! My voice would disappear by day five or six. I did not teach any more hours in Siyangi than I did elsewhere and yet it was my voice, the means to impart biblical truth, that was taken from me. I believe the enemies to the gospel were responsible in this instance.

We were not inclined to shrink back from going into the battle, although admittedly we did feel less enthusiasm in going to Siyangi than to any of the other villages. Yet we regularly knew more blessing at Siyangi than anywhere else. Each visit we made underlined the importance of being more prayerful than before, wiser to the powers counteracting our teaching. We made it a daily point to break, in the powerful name of Christ, any new curse being put on us or upon others who were growing in the Lord. Whilst laundering and bathing down in the river we had special times of prayer, for this was the only time we could be assured of being left on our own without interruption. We didn't mind the group of children who accompanied us, for they would soon tire of us and go off hunting for shrimps and small fish. Those riverside times became important, critical to the advance of the gospel in Siyangi, as we gave the best part of the afternoon to prayer and reflection, as well as getting on with those necessary chores and catching up with one another.

We also gave time every evening, before we closed our meetings, to ask for prayer requests. As these were many, I wrote them down as much a reminder to myself than for the reason of ticking off answered prayer. Each night we would read out the prayer requests from previous nights and asked the folk concerned for an update. Initially, most of the requests concerned health matters, children who had diarrhoea, a wife who had spells of dizziness or faintness, a festering wound on a man's leg, that kind of thing. The Lord gave healing, although the cynic among us would claim that many would have got well anyway. But we have seen a simple ailment turning into something far more major because of the insanitary conditions, the lack of medicine and the heat and humidity that would turn even a scratch into a festering wound. We were amazed at how graciously God was answering over half of those requests before the week's end, except, of course, for my deteriorating voice.

Pagan Buhid consider most illnesses to be caused by malevolent ancestral spirits, retribution for failing to give the prescribed food offerings or for breaking a taboo. To treat an ailment meant having to appease the offended spirits and this would be done foremost by interceding through chanting to the spirits of the dead and, failing that, by sacrificing a chicken, even a pig.

When they became Christian, the Buhid naturally prayed to God with a vigorous faith which God graciously answered in many instances. The Buhid certainly expected God to heal, and were not surprised by a sudden and miraculous answer to prayer, not that they always presumed that God would respond in that manner. Even when recovery was slow, the healing was likewise attributed to God: nothing was taken for granted or attributed to natural recovery. The Buhid Church naturally put into practice what James exhorts the sick to do:

"Is any one of you sick? He should call the elders of the church to pray over him and anoint him with oil in the name of the Lord. And the prayer offered in faith will make the sick person well; the Lord will raise him up." (James 5:14–15)

James encourages the sick to examine their spiritual lives, to put right whatever obstacle may have come between the sick person and the Lord: a sin to confess, or something neglected that should now be attended to. Sickness becomes a time of reflection, the enforced rest offering opportunity to look into the soul. This was not foreign to the Buhid either who came out of a belief system of cause and effect.

It was not long before many recognised Alexandra as a person through whom God healed. Many sick would seek her out or send a relative, if housebound, asking her to pray for them. Excited as we were by these signs of God's grace in direct response to prayer, we were also disturbed by their high regard for us, the reputation that our prayers were especially effective. Perhaps some of this reaction stems from their pagan background when the Buhid placed their trust in the skills of the shaman to intercede successfully with the spirit world.

We reminded them that it is God who heals and not the one who prays, encouraging them to place their faith in the Lord and not in man.

Neither Alexandra nor I had ever sought a healing ministry. Soberly we acknowledged many instances when God chose not to heal in response to our prayers. The ministry of healing has always remained secondary to our principal concern to see men and women come out of the darkness and into the light, and increasingly to receive more of that light. Healing, we felt, should not become something separate from the greater need of making God's salvation known. But then neither should healing be ignored.

Some missionaries are wary of praying for healing, fearing that if the desire of the patient is not met, that this will be bad publicity for the gospel! A ministry of compassion, unfortunately, can become limited to a medical concern. Whilst this may meet the bodily needs of an individual, those being treated are left thinking that God is far off, limited in power and not that interested in them.

Making bold claims for Christ as the Lord of all creation, able to save from the devil's clutches, able to forgive from all past misadventures and able to empower into a newness of life – such claims gain little credibility especially among a pagan people, unless they are substantiated by the miraculous as the demonstration of Christ's supremacy over the demonic and mastery over the physical. In the absence of modern medicine, animists have looked to demons to heal their sicknesses. Before beginning to believe in Christ, the animist first looks to see if Christ is more powerful than their known lords, for if He is not, then why should they abandon the spirits of the dead and incur their wrath? Who would keep them from suffering, tragedy and death itself if there were no saviour greater than the demons?

God is even more willing to bring restoration of health when we are testifying to the love and power of God among a people who do not yet believe in Him. It is wonderful for bearers of the Good News to see the gospel commending itself to the hearers and onlookers as people are healed and freed from demonic interference through prayer. God continues to accredit the message of Christ through miracles, done through his disciples.

These answered prayers were understandably a huge encouragement to the new Christians as well as to those whose expectations had dimmed over the years of the Christian life. The new believers were like the little children that Jesus referred to when illustrating the humble and trusting attitude that we should have when approaching God (Matthew 18:2–6). We were pleased when people's prayer requests went beyond the physical needs and started requesting help to overcome gambling temptations, or wisdom to understand the scriptures, or the ability to remember what they had learned, or expressing concern for an unbelieving spouse. It seemed to us that God delighted all the more in answering such requests. The church was growing, the teaching was nearly always well received – and yet I was still losing my voice at the end of a week. There was nothing for it but to go home. It puzzled me and still perplexes me now: why would God allow his mouthpiece to be silenced? Maybe the Siyangi church had reached, by day seven, a kind of saturation point in their ability to absorb spiritual truths?

When we left Siyangi after that first visit, the number of believers who accompanied us on the trail surprised us. We were used to having three or four companions to ensure we did not take the wrong trail and help to carry some of our bags, as well as to protect us from snakes and violent men, but twenty or so people?

As we progressed along the trail, we noticed that this lively party was diminishing, groups of three or four disappearing up one valley, another four crossing the river and starting on a trail that took them up to a concealed hamlet. And so the reduction continued until we only had three Buhid remaining with us when we reached the broken bridge from where we would board the jeepney back to our rented home in Bongabong.

We asked, where had the others gone to along these different trails?

"They are going to tell family and friends in those places what they have come to see and to believe!"

We had not told them to go, but the Spirit had compelled them to share this new-found joy with those who were near and dear. Excitement about God is by far the best impetus for evangelism.

* * *

Encouraging though these visits to Siyangi were, there had not been any decisions for baptism since these Buhid began turning to the Lord. I began asking why this was so, and received a variety of answers. One wag suggested that the Buhid did not want to pay the one peso weekly tithe, which all baptised members are supposed to give, according to their church constitution!

The root of the matter though was one of fear. According to their understanding, you could become a believer without inciting the wrath of the ancestral spirits. But once you were baptised, you had stated your change of allegiance, and became a target.

The situation was not helped by one of their teachers maintaining one day: "God persecutes those who are baptised!" The teacher scratched her head before continuing to voice her confusion: "I don't know why God persecutes the baptised when baptism is what He requires? He loves us and sometimes as a parent, we hit our children and the children don't always understand why!"

No wonder no one wanted to be baptised with the belief that all sorts of harm would fall upon the household: arguments, illness, curse upon the fields, all of which God brought about, seemingly in league with the demons!

It took careful instruction to explain why God *permits* persecution, the emphasis being on God allowing persecution to take place and understanding too that the agent carrying out the persecution was not God, but their new enemy the devil, who "prowls around like a roaring lion looking for someone to devour". The response was clear: to "be self-controlled and alert", to ". . . resist him, standing firm in the faith, because you know that your brothers throughout the world are undergoing the same kind of sufferings."

Passages like the opening chapter of Job, where God permits Satan to persecute Job within specified limits, went some way to aid their understanding that Satan can persecute but only within the restrictions God puts in place. There was more light when they realised that suffering encourages a dependency upon God and refines our character, putting us into the mould of the Lord Jesus. Through such suffering and fiery trials, our faithfulness may glorify Him who went before us, walking the way of the cross:

> "These [trials] have come so that your faith – of greater worth than gold, which perishes even though refined by fire – may be proved genuine and may result in praise, glory and honour when Jesus Christ is revealed." (1 Peter 1:7)

Once they grasped something of these truths and mysteries, they understood that God was not persecuting those who were baptised! Instead, as was the experience of a good many, God permitted the newly baptised to be tested. They began to understand that we must remain faithful and pure, and call out to the Lord in our distress, who comes graciously to equip us and see us through the dark valley of these times of suffering (1 Peter 5:8–10).

Some still needed convincing that God was all-powerful, that Satan was no match as he is only a created being, although an awesome force, as far as we are concerned. Others, who had no difficulty in believing that God is the Almighty One, wondered whether He would be mindful of them, a seemingly insignificant individual?

When the scriptures convinced them of an all-powerful and loving God who seeks a relationship with man, then they were prepared to be baptised and to face the consequences. First it was a group of nine, followed a couple of months later by a further nine, and within an eighteen-month period, about 30 men and women had been baptised in Siyangi alone.

CHAPTER SIX

THE STOLEN WORD

Blacksmith using bamboo bellows.

Glowing charcoals from the forge!

"Let my teaching fall like rain and my words descend like dew, like showers on new grass, like abundant rain on tender plants." (Deut.32:2)

"Martin! I have had a dream! Can you explain to me what it means?"

Bado was always the first, here in Siyangi, to come to the early-morning meeting at 6 a.m. He was clearly excited. I invited him to share his dream but cautioned him that not all dreams have obvious significance. If his dream was anything like one of Alexandra's, which she frequently regaled me with over breakfast, then he was not to expect me to make any sense out of it! Whilst Alexandra's dreams are highly entertaining, they are also quite preposterous. Dreams, I concluded, are quite often little more than the outworking of our wishes and worries, which when combined with the lively imagination that Alexandra has, could lead to all sorts of wild and fanciful conclusions if one were to interpret them.

Bado looked, understandably, a little crestfallen.

"Of course, on the other hand," I proceeded, realising that I had dampened his enthusiasm, "God has spoken to people through dreams in the Bible, like Joseph and Daniel, and their dreams were full of meaning and spoke of things still to come. So tell me your dream, and we can ask God to give us insight."

Bado ruffled his ample hair, making it even more dishevelled.

"In my dream, I was standing at the front of the church. I opened my Bible on the lectern and was turning the pages when suddenly the book turned to stone. What does it mean?"

"Well, tell me some more? What else did you see?" I pursued.

"That was it!" He grinned, awaiting my interpretation.

"Well there is nothing apparent that comes to my mind." I stroked my beard, thinking whether to pursue the matter further. "We should ask God perhaps if there is anything He wants to say to you, or to us, through this dream. He will reveal it if there is anything He wants us to know!"

We prayed briefly. There was no sudden revelation.

"Tell me, Bado," I continued, "was there anything written on the page of the Bible when it had turned to stone?"

"Oh yes!" he returned.

I released a silent hallelujah within me.

"Written on the page was James 1:5!"

Now whether it was the prayer that brought to mind the verse, or whether he overlooked what he considered an inconsequential detail, I do not know. But I was rejoicing that it had been this verse, for we had studied it as a group earlier that week. Bado often scratched his head over a text we were studying and often prayed for better understanding. He was keen to know God but his mind was quite dull. I asked Bado to turn up the reference in his Bible and to read it out:

"If any of you lacks wisdom, he should ask God, who gives generously to all without finding fault, and it will be given to him."

Bado smiled after he had stumbled through the verse.

"Do you believe in this promise?" I challenged him.

"Yes, I believe in all of God's promises. But," he hesitated and vigorously rearranged the thatch that made up his hair, "maybe this promise is not for me!"

"Bado – this verse is for the encouragement of all believers! Moreover, God has specifically reminded you of His promise in a vivid dream that you felt led to share with me. Now that has to be very much God's promise for you!"

Bado's amiable face broadened into an incredulous grin.

"As is true of the majority of God's promises, there is a condition that you first have to do before you can expect to get the promise. What is that condition in this verse?"

Bado looked intently. He soon said that if he were to receive wisdom, he was first to ask for it by praying.

I asked him, in so far as his own devotions went at home, did he make a point of praying before reading God's word? I was surprised when he said that he did not. I soon learned there were many others, like Bado, who avidly read the scriptures and were discouraged by not understanding much, or retaining little of what they had read. What I found in common with all these people was that none of them prayed for understanding. There are, of course, other reasons for failing to benefit much from our own reading of scripture, such as being in a hurry or having other things on your mind. But the problem was greater than could be explained by these obvious causes.

Jesus told the parable of the four soils (or "the sower" as it is more commonly known) to illustrate the spiritual dimension to this problem. The sower casts the seed on the field and some of it falls on the path where the ground is hard from the tread of many feet. It cannot enter into the ground and so the birds come along and peck it up. Jesus explained the meaning of this parable as follows:

> "The seed is the word of God. Those along the path are the ones who hear, and then the devil comes and takes away the word from their hearts, so that they may not believe and be saved." (Luke 8:11–12)

The seed, God's word, is so vital for the maturing process of the Christian. Knowing this, Satan is active in snatching that seed up before it germinates and takes root in our lives.

There was a distinct change when the Buhid started to pray before reading, asking for wisdom to be given to them.

When we returned to Siyangi, three months after the visit when Bado had been given his dream, he came up to me just as I was taking off my heavy pack, saturated with sweat.

"Oooh!" Bado let out a rising yelp of delight on seeing me, the finest greeting I have ever received.

"I am like a bamboo container," he continued. I looked quizzically at him, wondering what on earth he was on about.

"Before I had that dream, I was like an empty bamboo. Water had gone in and cleaned it but the water had escaped. But after the dream, when I started to ask God to give me understanding of His word and to make me wise, God began to add His living water into the tube, drip by drip, sometimes even a trickle, but usually just drip by drip."

I began to understand his analogy, for the Buhid used to gather water in bamboo sections. The wider sections could hold two or three pints of water. By cutting a length at one end just below the sealed seam and then cutting just below the seal at the next section up, this provided a foot to a foot-and-a-half-long tube, with a natural base and an open top through which to collect the spring water. A number of these would be carried together by means of a vine tied through holes specially bored through the tops of the bamboo sections. Nowadays, in the Buhid villages within easier access to the temporary markets, like the one at Lisap, the Buhid collect water in plastic buckets. The Buhid of the interior, the Bangon, still gather their water in the manner to which Bado was referring.

"Once I was empty, but now I am no longer a bamboo container that rattles hollow, for the Lord is filling me!" concluded Bado, his face aglow with the wonder of what God was doing.

Bado never missed a single teaching session and began asking some searching questions. He and his friend Anaw would often seek me out during the late afternoon or late evening after the teaching session and sooner or later their jovial interchanges with one another turned to the gospel. There was a passage they had read: could I explain what it meant? Or there was a matter bothering them about which they wanted to know whether our Father's word had something to say. These men were growing in spiritual stature.

Mighty is God's word. I have witnessed the word growing on a person, giving him a desire to read more, a thirst that is satisfied by further reading, a thirst that strangely warms the heart and yet never cloys the appetite for more. Onward goes the pilgrim through the unexplored pages of his Bible with a seeking spirit that will not rest until he has found his answer.

At various turns he sees his Lord, exalted and lifted up through the smoke that fills the temple, shaken to its foundations by His presence; the resplendent One waited upon by fearsome and mysterious angelic beings. At another turn, he sees his Lord humble, becoming a baby, needing the nursing hand of a mother and yet still the object of veneration as wise men travel the vast and lonely desert expanses of the east to come and worship Him. At another turn, the pilgrim sees the power and wrath of the Lord calling the world to account, having patiently given time for repentance. He now moves with dreadful judgement, raining fire down on Sodom and Gomorrah. How even more wonderful then becomes that figure, writing with his finger in the dust, whilst an adulteress's accusers walk away under the weight of their own unrighteousness and he mercifully says: "Go now and leave your life of sin!"

God's word is irresistible, like the flashing of a sharp scimitar cutting the air – emphasising the compelling nature of the word of God – a sharpness that cuts through our torpor and separates all that is pretentious from what is true and of lasting value.

Anaw was my host, a man I had first met in the back of a kariton (a solid-wheeled bullock cart), bumping along the boulder-strewn flood plain to Siyangi, his face expressing the post-operative pain after an appendectomy three days earlier. To look at him back then, one would never have thought he was made of the stuff needed to become a spiritual leader. He liked playing the fool, acting dumb, and had a silly laugh together with a foolish voice he would put on, which could get on your nerves after a while. You would not have credited him with much intelligence at all, but nevertheless he made an amenable host, allowing us to sleep in his spare house to the side of his own. He had a strict wife who often moaned about how inept he was in doing any task beyond the ken of a farmer. I felt sorry for him.

But becoming a man or woman of God does not depend on the stuff that we are made of. It is not of ourselves, not through our doing, but by the grace of God that we can become what God desires all Christians to become, once we have made God our desire and seized hold of Him never to let go. The maturing was not for his own edification alone, but was beginning to benefit the whole church:

> "We will in all things grow up into him who is the head, that is, Christ. From him the whole body, joined and held together by every support- ing ligament, grows and builds itself up in love, as each part does its work." (Ephesians 4:15–16)

To see Anaw now, one could be forgiven for thinking that he was entirely another person, such had been his transformation in Christ. I had no part in this. He was not the kind of protégé that Bado had become for me. Anaw had looked so unpromising that I confess I held no aspirations for him. But at some point, between my visits, he had crossed over that dividing line, and decided to make his life count for the Lord. Anaw could well have made Christ his Lord on another occasion many years ago, when he and his wife went to the Mangyan Bible School. They had lasted a single term there only, coming home again to Siyangi, never to return. Now fully committed to Christ, he still retained his playfulness, but it was somehow different than before, not demeaning, but rather endearing. He had now imposed a limit to his lightheartedness, recognising that taken to its former extreme, it had made him look foolish and would now bring dishonour to His Lord.

Anaw is an inspiring example of what God can do with a man, or alternatively, what man can do for himself by getting serious with God. God stands at the door ready to enter into our lives, to fellowship with us, and the onus rests upon us as to whether we will let Him in, and to allow Him to speak to us about our shortcomings and the possibilities that can be gained through faith.

When observing Inggoy, the blacksmith, at work one day in Batangan, it came to me how like the fashioning of a fotol (the machete that all Buhid carry) is the making of a man of God. Inggoy starts with a thickish piece of iron, a sort of short rail, perhaps some fourteen inches in length and a quarter of an inch thick. Such an implement cannot cut and is of no use even in the most skilled of hands. First the blacksmith builds up his charcoal fire, blowing air through the bamboo tubes that make up the bellows, until the forge is glowing red. He places the useless piece of metal in the fire until it too is red hot. Removing it with a large pair of pincers, he takes the glowing metal over to his anvil, aims a few well-aimed blows on the metal with his hammer in quick succession, then returns it to the fire again. This he patiently repeats for some three hours, all the time the metal is taking shape from being heavy, clumsy and blunt, to becoming a recognisable fotol, gently curved, with a keen edge down one side, gracefully coming to a sharp point.

We come into the Christian life with nothing to commend ourselves, and God begins His work on us. Becoming a sharp, gracefully fashioned fotol, of use in the hand of God, will entail the fire and the hammer. Without allowing the fiery trials to shape us, we will remain blunt and of little use in the Kingdom.

On another visit to Siyangi, perhaps a year after Bado told me his dream, he came to the front of the church when I concluded the meeting in prayer. It was the Sunday night, the last night of my visit. Bado cleared his throat and announced:

"We don't need our faduwasay!" "Faduwasay" is a Buhid term meaning "brother", which I asked them to use instead of the somewhat more elevated Tagalog title they had previously used of "kuya" , meaning "big brother".

I looked up, quite taken aback. This was the goal towards which we were aiming, to work ourselves out of a job by training capable leaders, but this announcement, I felt, was somewhat premature.

Bado stood there grinning, and ruffled his hair so much in his embarrassed confusion that it stood up on end. "What I mean is that when Faduwasay Martin is here in Siyangi, we study the Bible morning and night." Here he paused, looking around the church at the sea of faces waiting to hear what he was going to say next.

"I don't know about the rest of you, but come tomorrow morning, I will be here in the church to start reading Genesis. If anyone wants to come and join me, I will be glad because you might be able to explain a verse that I don't understand. And who knows," here he paused like a good actor, although there was nothing contrived about his manner, "I might even be able to explain something to you!"

Thus began a twice-daily Bible study and prayer time, inaugurated by Bado. Bado's dream had something of the prophetic about it, for he was standing at the front of the church with an open Bible in his dream, a foresight of his leading the church in these devotions.

Numbers were not impressive at these Bible studies, but a faithful core of some five to eight folk were in attendance and often attracted others who were not so committed. Studying the Bible on your own has its limitations when there are no devotional guides, nor commentaries or Bible dictionaries to refer to. The knowledge available to the Buhid was spread among the keen Christians and so it was in their best interests to pool that knowledge by having a communal quiet time. The discussions stemmed from the passage being studied, but this was often a springboard to consult parallel texts when appropriate, or to look up different texts that related to the issue under discussion. I was surprised how much benefit each acquired from this method. The more that they read, the greater became their resources of reference in interpreting scripture. So they used scripture to interpret scripture, the sound basis of all exegesis. They would make a mental note of meanings that still remained hidden, and would question me about them on my next visit. Sometimes when I was not able to give as full an answer as either they or I would wish, I had the resources to consult and bring them a considered answer next time.

We equipped every church with a concordance and showed them how these worked. It appealed to the preachers among them, but we were disappointed that others did not make use of them as well. To the Siyangi church, we gave a two-volume edition of a commentary through the whole New Testament in Tagalog, as this was the one large church that did not have a graduate from the Mangyan Bible School. Again we were disappointed they made little use of this also, perhaps contrasting the difference between our academic orientation and ability as individuals to extract information from book sources, with their preference for group participation and ability to listen more and learn from one another. They found solitary academic pursuit unnatural.

Their ability to learn without a trained teacher, mixed with their reticence to use Bible aids stemming from their non-literary background, reminded me of part of the prophecy concerning the coming Holy Spirit in Jeremiah.

"'I will put my law in their minds and write it on their hearts. I will be their God, and they will be my people. No longer will a man teach his neighbour, or a man his brother, saying "Know the Lord", because they will all know me, from the least of them to the greatest', declares the Lord". (Jeremiah 31:33–34)

I am not advocating that this is the ideal way, to rely solely on the Holy Spirit and not listen to trained teachers. But I do commend this approach of being keen to get acquainted with the word of the Lord. Having a hunger to read the scriptures systematically in whole portions is likely to bring a far greater maturity in an individual, than reading much of our Christian literature with our penchant for following Bible study aids. Similarly it is better than reading scripture snippets and listening to teachers who are highly selective in their preaching with their own agendas, preferences and prejudices. It is a salutary reminder for us to weigh in the balance all of what we are reading and listening to, and to take an honest look at our own thirst for God and progress along the path of holiness. With all our resources, and some of these are excellent, we ought to be progressing more spiritually than our brothers and sisters who live in parts of the world deprived of books and computer technology. But the contrary is often the case.

The church was making great strides. And yet there were times of poor attendance, particularly at the Sunday afternoon service. When we came to a church like Siyangi, there were very few Bibles available, perhaps as few as four or five in a village of 35 households. The Bible study course that we ran during our first visit had a scheme, whereby for the fee of what was then the equivalent of 50 pence, they could get a Bible complete with Old Testament by returning their completed answer-workbook to the Bible League. Over 200 Buhid households took advantage of this scheme. It was a joy to see the Buhid save up their few pesos to buy themselves a Bible, and a greater joy to see evidence of these being much read, not so much by noting the tattered state of their Bibles, but rather by the fact that meaningful passages had been underlined freehand. Some Buhid would have the habit of turning over the corners of the pages that they had read, thus making a bulky Bible, distorting the book's spine. They soon became filthy through being well thumbed by the fireside, where ash and charcoal coated them. A well-thumbed Bible missing its cover is a good sight, better by far than an ornate one that remains on the shelf.

We brought in other literature, such as Bible cartoon-comics: an effective way to get the semi-literate started. By the time they had finished reading all twelve or so comics in the series, they were then ready for reading the Bible. Here the Buhid needed some guidance as to where to begin, as well as to know where to find the characters they had grown to love from the comics. Those who progressed on from reading about the heroes of the faith wanted to know how to go about reading large portions of the Bible without getting bogged down in lengthy genealogies, or descriptions of tabernacle furnishings and priestly garments. All the Bible reading schemes on the market in the Philippines that I sifted through were either too comprehensive, too incomplete, or jumped around the Bible too much. So I compiled one to suit those starting off in their reading adventure in the Bible, majoring on the story element, bringing a mixture from both Old and New Testaments. I did not provide notes, only simple headings for each reading, providing the theme of what the passage was about.

Every year, the Buhid stage a conference for their tribal group of churches. These events are the highlight of the year, for more reasons than spending three consecutive days and four nights studying the Bible and singing praise songs. At these festive gatherings, the young meet with the youth from other villages and marriages are sometimes the consequence.

It was Siyangi's turn to host the conference and they had wanted us to arrange to bring in a film projector and generator to show the "Jesus" film in Tagalog. Siyangi is strategically located for reaching many villages and hamlets, and even the sub-tribe of the Bangon, none of which had had a Christian witness for years, if ever. Many of the Siyangi Christians came from all kinds of places from the back of beyond up in the hills and had married spouses who had grown up in Siyangi. With their new-found excitement in the Lord, they went back to their places of origin and encouraged their folks to come and see the great film to be shown in Siyangi. When the day of the conference arrived, entire families came down from the hinterland and set up camp about the church building.

Great excitement was in the air. Although the rear wall panel had been removed from the church and an extension added, it was still hopelessly small for the 300 or so who had gathered.

After the conference, we urged the church to follow up those who had come to see the film. A good number of them came from Sigaw, another half-hour's walk upriver, and it was our prayer that we might be able to gather a number of people in that place and begin a church.

On our next visit to Siyangi some three months later, I asked whether I could be taken to Sigaw, especially since no real concerted effort had been made to evangelise the village. But it was not possible due to a rebel camp in the vicinity. Seeing my disappointment, Buhadan cheered me up by saying: "You can't go, but we can!"

And so began a weekly outreach every Friday morning to Sigaw, where banana buyers and the like came from the lowlands and Buhid and Bangon came down from their mountain fastnesses, to avoid the extra two-and-a-half-hour walk that would be entailed if they were to sell their produce at Lisap at the Saturday market. The Siyangi Christians took with them coloured posters of drawings depicting Bible scenes, using these as a cue to tell the gospel message. These pictures had been carefully stored, rolled up and kept in a dry corner of Anaw's house. When one of these attractive pictures was unrolled on the market corner, a crowd would gather round, listening for a while, interrupting on occasions to clarify a detail. Hardly any of them stayed the full length of the explanation, but resolutely turned their back, spat a copious stream of saliva reddened by the chewing of betel nut onto the ground and walked away.

For six months, the Siyangi church went every Friday with their posters and zealously shared the gospel, but no one showed a lasting interest. One couple did say they wanted to follow this new teaching, but were never seen again. The church members became demoralised and ceased going. I comforted them, commending them for their faithfulness, and drew their attention to God's declaration in Isaiah:

"As the rain and snow come down from heaven and do not return to it without watering the earth and making it bud and flourish, so that it yields seed for the sower and bread for the eater, so is my word that goes out from my mouth: It will not return to me empty, but will accomplish what I desire and achieve the purpose for which I sent it." (Isaiah 55:10–11)

The seed is sown and will not be entirely lost. Although no one turned to the Lord in Sigaw, the time will come when they will.

CHAPTER SEVEN

THE VEIL

"Where are you off to?" I greeted Rufeno, a young Hanunoo man who had married a Buhid girl. They had been living in Batangan for several years now.

"Just across the river to cut some bamboo. Are you cooking breakfast?" Rufeno stopped on the other side of the wattle fence that had in part become a hedge. The straight branches pushed into the ground to mark the allotment that came with the Hanselmans' former house in Batangan, had mostly been still green with sap and had amazingly taken root and come into bud and leaf.

"No," I replied, "I am just boiling water for some coffee. Are you in a hurry? Would you like a cup?" I lifted the lid up slightly from the cooking pot on the fire with a short stick, checking whether it had reached a simmer. It had not, but air bubbles were beading the inside walls of the pot.

"Probably not!" Rufeno looked across the river to the jungle on the far side where the large bamboo were growing.

We carried on an exchange of pleasantries, asking after each other's children's health, the maize planting and such like. The conversation reached a halt and Rufeno looked keen to go. I smiled at him, wishing him well.

"Well, I'll probably be on my way then," he announced. I raised my chin in acknowledgement of his departure and looked down to attend to the fire.

"Do dreams have a meaning?" Rufeno asked, having taken a couple of paces before halting again beside the fence.

Remembering Bado's prophetic dream, I was not going to be quite so dismissive again and spoke about how God spoke to some through dreams in the Bible. I asked whether he had had a specific dream in mind and would he like to share it with me and if we could ask the Lord whether it had any significance.

"I dreamt that I was at home looking out of the window, just where the path divides into two," he began to relate his dream with that careful attention that characterised his whole person. Rufeno was handsome, almost feminine with his soft features, and yet strong as all tribal folk are.

"You and 'Xandra were there, all dressed in white, long flowing white garments. You were standing beside a large white cross that was raised right at the centre of the division in the path."

Rufeno sometimes came to church but he was quite sporadic in his attendance. Once he had shared during the testimony slot, when we were still new to the Buhid work, how he was not sure whether he really was a disciple of the Lord Jesus or not. That was the only time I had seen him up at the front. To my shame, I never followed him up, excusing myself with the thought that someone else who knew him and already had a relationship would speak with him. Shortly after he declared his doubts, I did invite him to help me with the youth group that met at our house on Friday nights, as I would be glad to have his skill as a guitarist. But he had said that he was not the right person and that he probably would not be of any use to me.

Whether the interpretation of Rufeno's dream was obvious, or the Lord gave me immediate understanding, I don't quite know.

"I believe your dream to have meaning. I believe the Lord is speaking to you," I began. "Your spiritual journey has come to a standstill. You have arrived at a fork in the trail. One way leads down to the river, the other up into the hills and jungle. You don't know which way to take.

"The cross is all important in this dream, for it stands at the parting of ways, at the very point of this decision. You cannot ignore it, for there is a choice to be made about Jesus who died on that cross to open up a way for you to come to God."

"What about you and Xandra dressed in white?" he asked.

"We are in white only because Jesus has taken our sins away and we are clothed in His righteousness. We probably feature in your dream because the Lord has sent us to this place to show the way of salvation. That is why we are standing by the cross to explain its meaning to you and to others."

Rufeno was quiet, apparently satisfied with the explanation and lost in thought. Surely God was speaking very specifically to him.

I asked Rufeno whether he would like me to come to his home later that day so we could do a simple Bible study together that would more satisfactorily explain the way of salvation.

"I probably will not understand!" Rufeno excused himself. I replied that we would go at a slow pace, that it would be just the two of us and I would make sure he understood what he read because God was very obviously wanting him to hear. He made one or two other excuses. I got the impression that these were not excuses of reluctance, but rather he feared he might be wasting my time as he considered himself slow in understanding. He eventually was persuaded it would be quite all right for me to visit him, for after all this was the reason why we had come to Batangan, and that he would not be wasting my time.

I came to his home late that afternoon. Rufeno was a little apprehensive. I tried to put him at ease with some small talk, but he was clearly worried about whether he would be able to understand anything from the Bible. We prayed first, specifically for clarity and spiritual illumination. The study took a long time for I tried, largely unsuccessfully, to draw out answers from him. Sometimes he just remained silent, and it would be apparent that he was not going to answer. I spoon-fed him, summarised the main points of the text we had studied and prayed with him again before I left him.

We repeated our one-to-one Bible study sessions every day for the remaining days of our stay. Rufeno began to feel less embarrassed about my giving him my complete attention. His reading improved together with his ability to actually try to answer all my questions. The Lord was clearing a mental blockage there, or maybe it was a spiritual blindness, a web of deceit he had become entangled in made by the one who is "the father of lies" (John 8:44). I encouraged him at the end of that stay in Batangan, to continue reading through Mark's gospel. Although he appeared a little more confident, I did wonder how determined he would be to carry on, given his scepticism about his own mental abilities. Rufeno became a subject for daily prayer and we brought his situation to the attention of prayer partners back home.

Three months passed as we made a round of the other Buhid churches before we returned to Batangan. No sooner had we arrived on our balcony ready to remove our shoes before unlocking the house, than Rufeno joined us. To visit someone who has just arrived is considered slightly bad form, for the Buhid usually like to lie down and rest when they have arrived at a place. We knew there was something he wanted to tell us sooner rather than later.

We sat down together on the bench and, having politely asked after the health of his household, I queried how he had got on with his reading through Mark's gospel.

Rufeno was beaming. He had managed to read through the whole gospel, he informed me proudly. Then he announced: "I have been able to give up gambling!"

I asked if anyone had told him to give it up? No, no one had, but he knew that gambling on the cock fighting was inconsistent with this new life he now had. We studied some more together that week and I was joyful that the former doubter, who believed himself incapable of understanding the basic Bible message, had moved on from those lies and now had eyes opened to the truth.

Rufeno's story did not continue like Bado's testimony of growing in the Lord and becoming a leader in the church. I am sure the potential was there, but the difference between one who continues to grow, and one whose spiritual life plateaus, boils down to a matter of the human will, for God is always willing to bring us through to maturity. Rufeno's story illustrates how God was specifically leading certain people on through divine intervention, in the form of dreams, as well as revealing the pall of spiritual doubt and oppression Satan casts over a community.

*　*　*

One day, sitting on our balcony in Batangan with Buhid friends, I happened to remark that since it was mango season, why were there so few mangoes on a large tree that grew near the house.

"It hasn't been worked!" said an old man with a staccato laugh, revealing the one front tooth that remained in his mouth. "You know that tree was from a mango that Roberto had eaten and had passed it on to be planted!"

"What do you mean by 'working' a tree?" I asked him.

"You see," the old man explained, eager to inform the ignorant missionary, "from the time the new fruit appears on the tree, we gather dry leaves under the tree and make a bonfire. Once it is lit, we put some wet leaves on top and that makes quite a smoke that goes up into the tree's branches. All the grubs that are feeding on the tree and on its fruit either drop off or fly away because of the choking smoke."

"And how often do you have to do that?" Alexandra asked.

"Every day until the fruit is ready for picking!" The old man laughed good-humouredly again.

I thought about this process of ensuring fruitfulness in terms of plenty and quality and saw in it a parable of spiritual fruitfulness. We cannot expect fruit to appear by doing nothing about it. We have the potential to produce spiritual fruit. Our fruitfulness is in part a mystery, a God-given quality that we have no means of manufacturing ourselves. But we do have the potential to spoil the fruit, or even to stop it from appearing through allowing sin to do what it will, unchecked in our lives. That sin is like the grubs that spoil the fruit. Sin is dealt with through the reading of the word and its application, like the gathering of the leaves and the smoke from the fire. It needs to be a daily process to ensure fruitfulness, large mangoes that are wholesome and tasty.

The Batangan church was like that mango tree, large and impressive to look at, promising much, but with so little fruit on it.

Batangan was a place where you could be preaching or teaching and although people were quiet and facing you, with Bibles open in their hands, you could sometimes see a veil come over their faces, a veil keeping them from understanding the word. All seemed to lapse into a daydream for long intervals. More than a case of losing interest, or of being indifferent to the message, the attention lapse came over those who were keen for the Lord, who were attending the weekday sessions. This was not just our perception alone, for Ernesto had commented on this after a visit he made when he had preached to a totally unresponsive congregation. It was not boredom, for Ernesto was a natural storyteller, mingling good humour with spiritual content, and yet they did not take note of him.

We determined that it must be a spiritual veil coming from the darkness. We directed prayer against it, but it still persisted in descending now and then.

I got the impression that for many of those who had been in the Christian life for a number of years, they felt they had arrived at the goal of their faith and they only had to maintain what they were already doing up until then, which usually meant abstaining from committing anything on their own list of wrongs. They lacked the real desire to grow, marked by a holy dissatisfaction with what they were. They had no great expectations of God beyond the wish to receive their daily needs and answered prayer for health concerns. This stuck-in-a-rut type of Christianity, self-righteous in its own defence, caused apathy, loss of vision to live daringly for the Lord and to take the gospel to the many unreached places.

Monay and his wife Talad worked closely with us. They would share all that was on their hearts concerning the condition of the church, questions that had been raised, issues that remained unresolved, and the confusion caused by outside denominations coming in with their own particular emphasis, presented in a way to deliberately make the Buhid Christians feel inferior.

There is always the danger of becoming partisan in defence of mainstream evangelical views, to put God's revelation into a box, neatly packaged and parcelled up. But of course it is not in the nature of God to be so easily defined and determined. God cannot be tamed: He is bigger than any of our theologies. In preparing a seminar about the Holy Spirit, I was aware of both my own limitations as well as those of the Buhid, in our experience of the Holy Spirit. Surely we were to remain open to God, in His dealing with us in ways beyond our present experience of Him, and yet in a manner that was still compatible with scripture. I encouraged the Buhid that we were to thirst for more of God and to desire spiritual gifts as the church is encouraged to do (1 Corinthians 12:31 & 14:1).

These issues arising from both within the church and the community as well as those issues coming from churches outside clearly needed to be addressed. I was never at a loss as to what to preach or teach about. Many of the topics required a seminar type of approach, extending over a period of a week or more. It was both a joy and a challenge to me to prepare these materials, since I was particularly keen to present the teaching in whole text sections rather than verses in isolation. That way, the fuller counsel of God was obtained, presented in the context in which it appears in the Bible. This made it easier for the Buhid to remember.

The teaching was well received and understood at times, and an animated question session would emerge. Then we would feel on the verge of a breakthrough until that veil fell once again, taking most of the Buhid in Batangan captive. Only the occasional individual did not succumb to this spiritual lethargy; people like Monay and his wife Talad were immune.

Once, after preaching one Sunday morning, when there were definite signs of people having taken in God's word and being warmed by it, I went back to our home feeling drained as usual. There was the lunch to put together as Alexandra had got caught up with pastoral and health concerns back at the church. I decided first to have a quiet five minutes on the back step of the house. A high, raised bamboo screen around the top of the steps, concealed me from those passing along the path that ran alongside the river and past our house, making it a good place to have those five minutes. Although I was tired, I was pleased by their responsiveness that morning.

To my side lay a fotol, sheathed in a scabbard. I felt my hand drawn towards it and the thought stormed my mind: "Put an end to your life!" It would be easy, I could slash my wrists deeply, let the blood drain into one of the large buckets that we kept on the back step, so no one would be suspicious on seeing a trickle of blood fall through the bamboo slats. With an appalling sense of horror, I saw my arm move by a will of its own for the fotol. I did not seem able to retract it. Guessing what was happening, I called out to the Lord. The spell was broken.

A few minutes later, Monay passed by, most unusually at that time after the service. He did not have any business but felt drawn to visit me. I shared with him what had happened. He did not show surprise but understood immediately the powers of darkness that were operating, opposing the proclamation of the truth that threatened the reign of evil. Monay led in prayer. I was so glad to have had Christian fellowship just at that moment and soon Alexandra came and joined in the prayer time.

One could have argued that the reason for this spiritual indifference in Batangan was due to many of the Buhid being worldly wise, showing signs of doing their share of wheeling and dealing. With the main market day in the Philippines falling on a Sunday, the pursuit of business had a big effect on church attendance. Three jeepneys ran in and out of the place with sackloads of copra, coffee and avocados, star apples and maize, great lengths of bamboo, bags of charcoal and huge clusters of bananas. Everyone who had the will to be industrious could find plenty of demand for whatever grew. The folk of Batangan no longer waited for the middlemen to come to buy their produce; the Buhid now owned three jeepneys to take their produce direct to the traders in the Roxas market place an hour away.

Another rational argument to explain the spiritual apathy was the effect of having so many unbelievers about the town. The centre of the town was almost entirely populated by Luktanon who ran all the shops and eateries where small grubby bowls of boiled fish were served on cheap grey tinted rice. Few were God-fearing individuals. On the far side of Batangan were the animistic Buhid, some of whom professed allegiance to the Roman Catholic Church but still carried on with their spirit worship practices.

Much crime went on, stealing was very common, drunkenness on the increase, and many with gambling debts were plunged further into drink and even drugs. Prostitution was actively going on and cases of rape or attempted rape, even on very young girls came to our attention. Batangan had all the vice one would associate with the big city, but more alarming because it took place in a town of probably little more than 150 households.

The Christians had their own part of the town and it certainly did not feel threatening to be visiting there. But the evil atmosphere was most tangible in going across to the other side. Some areas felt extremely dark and accursed. We wondered what had taken place there or was still in progress – Satan felt as though he had a particular seat in that side of town, like the town of Pergamum – "where Satan has his throne" (Revelation 2:13). Neither we, nor the gospel message, ever made an impact over there, our prayers seemingly having no effect.

Some Christians were showing a growing interest in observing superstitions. Monay came to us one day disturbed by what had happened in the household of one of the church elders. The elder's wife was having difficulty giving birth. She had been in labour a long time but the baby seemed to be blocked. Monay had been called for and he had prayed for the wife and baby. They waited, but the labour continued without letting up, showing no signs whatsoever of coming to a conclusion. The elder, following the superstitious tradition of removing an item that was inside something else, then took the back off his radio to remove the batteries. Within minutes, the baby was delivered. The Christian parents attributed the birth, the clearance of the blockage, to the removal of the batteries from the radio.

"Why did God allow that to happen just at that time?" asked Monay, stung with righteous indignation and jealous for the honour of the Lord.

We had no answer for him for it was beyond our understanding. God had His reasons, but just then we felt as confused as Monay.

* * *

Christa was a newly-married girl whose parents asked me to see her, as she was deeply distressed within herself. She began to tell me her tale, with her parents and husband elaborating on it.

"When I try to go to church," the young girl started in her small and faltering voice, "two strangers meet me on the way and tell me that I am not to go. I follow them and they take me away out of town into the jungle. There I get hurt . . ." Christa broke off with visible anxiety across her face, her arms stiffening at the painful recollection.

"The strangers aren't people that I know," she continued in answer to our question, "they are not Buhid, nor Hanunoo, more Luktanon. They are unlike anyone I have ever met and they have power over me and I no longer can do what I want to do. What they say that I have to do!"

"She comes back from the forest," interjected her mother, "covered with bruises and cuts. One time she threw herself down from a low cliff and hurt her back. It still isn't right!"

"They forced me to jump off!" defended Christa pitifully.

"There are times when she is wild," shared Nilo, her husband. He pointed his chin in his father-in-law's direction as though to say, "Ask him". "It took four of us to hold her down to prevent her from harming herself!"

Many Buhid girls are strong, doing their share of the work in the fields and carrying home firewood and heavy baskets filled with bananas or sweet potatoes, but Christa's frame was extremely slight. She looked incapable of doing normal work, let alone needing four strong men to subdue her. Much of what she shared, spoke of the demonic, particularly as such visitations and super-human strength came over her at the time of the full moon. She complained of severe headaches too especially at that time.

Apparently, before she had married, Christa had been quite a normal, healthy girl, never seeing these spirit beings or coming under their influence. She had married into a family that dealt heavily in the occult. Her husband's father was a medium, as were her own mother's parents.

I asked Christa to read out to me the first chapter of Ephesians, on the principle that someone who was possessed of a demon or demons would be unable to read scripture that particularly exulted Christ as Lord and Saviour. I observed her carefully as she read. Christa had no problem reading through the whole chapter, but she confessed to being unable to pray, for no sooner had she begun than a severe headache would bring her to an abrupt halt. I concluded she was not possessed but went through times of being demonised. I said that we would pray, lay hands on her and anoint her with oil for the healing of her back and general weak constitution. Monay and Talad were the ones who anointed with oil and prayed for healing.

The following Sunday, Christa came to church. What a victory that must have been for her. Her non-believing husband, Nilo was there by her side, curious to learn more about the Christ in whose powerful name we had prayed.

We mentioned Christa and Nilo's circumstances to our prayer partners for this young couple to be specially upheld. Christa continued to come to church with Nilo. I did Bible studies with them once or twice in their home, but these did not continue as they were often away in Hanunoo land visiting Nilo's parents and working some land that Nilo had there. The headaches at full moon became a thing of the past, as too the unwelcome strangers. Our only concern was that she looked anaemic following the birth of their first child. We gave her some iron tablets and vitamins to help build her up. We felt the worst was well behind her, and it was only a question of time and she would pick up.

How wrong we were.

Monay, the man saved by a sneeze, with his wife Talad.

*Buhadan, sharing from a Bible comic. This gifted evangelist was
used in the dramatic birth of the Baliya Fontan church.*

Gano built us a surprise house. To his left is Deborah who was once injured by a spirit bowman.

Bado at his baptism. "Once I was empty but now I am no longer a bamboo container that rattles hollow because the Lord is filling me!"

*Waydinan with his wife Ignay. The small breakthrough
in the mission to Datag Bonglay followed the incident where
Waydinan offered the other cheek.*

For a year at Anaw, Samwil and Ibilin endured hardships for the sake of the gospel, including blankets wet from a leaking roof.

The Haworths (centre) with some of their Buhid family at Batangan.

Isaias singing the Going Home song:
"A man who makes a difference, whose
absence is sorely apparent".

Hogday and Kaw-kaw at home in Manihala. "Although they might t-t-torture me, I would not deny Christ," said Hogday.

Sayna (with his family), the leader of the small church at Safang Uyang. The gospel light had penetrated the fearful darkness.

CHAPTER EIGHT

AN ADVANCE

Underneath the frangipani tree, the elder groped for the short, thick metal rod in the fork of the trunk, shining his weak torch to locate it. Taking it up, he directed the torch to a long, rectangular plate of steel suspended from one of the branches and struck it several times. This was the church "bell". It gave a dull but solid clang that could be heard right up the river valley.

The Batangan church was especially full on this particular night. A special meeting had been called, attended not only by the Christians in Batangan, but also by a large contingent coming from Apnagan, headed by Diokno and his older brother Danggin. This date had been set at the recent conference held in Siyangi, where the presence of many pagan Buhid coming to see the film had brought about a missionary conviction.

Six couples had been identified (not all of them had volunteered) as being willing to relocate to a new area to start another church. All six couples were there, hailing from three different Buhid villages. The atmosphere was expectant, everyone's faces around the church looked wakeful, many beaming, keen to take in those present and to locate one or more friends.

It was proposed that each of the six husbands should come to the front to say a few words about the Lord's guidance.

"Brothers and sisters," began the first, the eldest man of all the six couples, with a distinctive head of curly, almost frizzy hair that was going grey. He made a lengthy preamble, referring to several of the folk present, the conversations he had had with them, but these friendly snippets, vaguely interesting as they might have been, said very little at all about God's calling. This was all by way of introduction, the preamble, of getting into the right mood, of feeling comfortable before a crowd and giving time for the congregation to tune in to his particular way of thinking. Only then, having dispensed with the preliminaries, did he come to the point: "Ginimay and I are willing to go, even though we are getting on in years. All our children have married and we are free to go. But we don't want to stay away for long periods. Maybe a week at a time and then we would come home, and then perhaps we could give another week. Something like that. We are old in years and I am not very quick at reading, but I am willing, with the Lord's help, to do and say what I can!"

He stood at the wobbly lectern, a post sunk into the earthen floor of the church, on top of which three short parallel planks had been nailed to a frame. Smiling, with open mouth and twinkling eyes, he looked as though he was going to say something more, but finding nothing to add, he sat down rather sheepishly.

The next of the six candidates was called forward. This man was probably twenty years the junior of the previous one. He wore a very ripped T-shirt, stained grey over most of the front with banana tree sap. This candidate had sleepy-looking eyes and stood there smiling for a moment or two, not quite knowing how to begin. Again he only came to the substance of what he had on his heart to share after a lengthy preamble.

"Perhaps we are not the best couple to choose, but then it depends on the Lord doesn't it, not on us? If He chooses, then we will go! But my wife would rather like to remain here in Batangan – all our children are here. . ." He stopped and broke out into a short laugh, loud and abrupt, telling of his embarrassment.

"You can take them with you!" shouted someone from the middle of the church, in the spirited tone of a heckler, a good-hearted heckler, but still with that unmistakable tone of one who intends to have some fun at another's expense. "None of them are married yet and they would be a help in the fields!"

"Yes, maybe," replied the one at the front, scratching his hair vigorously in his discomfort.

Another man was called forward, one of the younger ones. He was particularly well groomed and looked very intelligent. His whole poise suggested that he took great care in all he said or did. He spoke clearly and was not as circuitous as his predecessors in coming to the point:

"Look here, brothers, you are not to choose me. I am not that happy to go. It was not really me who put my name forward, but somebody else and that was done without properly asking me beforehand. It is true that I am a graduate from the Bible school, but so are some of the others. I think that I am to stay teaching in Apnagan, for the Lord has not spoken to me about going somewhere else. As I said, my going is someone else's idea, not mine – so don't choose me!"

He sat down quite abruptly, indicating something of the passion he felt. There was a little muttering around the church. Looking round, I caught sight of Monay. His face exhibited a vague suggestion of displeasure, a look that would have been missed in the blinking of an eye.

Another two came forward in the usual self-deprecating manner, both giving reasons more for their unworthiness in becoming missionaries, rather than speaking of their willingness to go. It appeared that the evening was going to be a farce, with such shows of humility making one wonder whether there would be any outcome at all.

How different were these candidates from those in the West, taught to sell their skills, to show themselves in a favourable light, outlining strengths and gifts and relevant experience and, in so doing, often drawing too much attention to themselves. Western interview skills can verge on the arrogant, particularly in the church context. There is often too little credence given to the truth that our worth rests not in so many accomplishments and academic ability, but rather on our ability to humble ourselves before the Lord and cry out for His enabling.

If we acknowledge our weakness in prayer, the strength of the Lord may then be demonstrated. Then our service can demonstrate the glory of the Lord, for the power is so evidently from Him and not of ourselves. Paul remarks that God's servant is only like a clay jar, a common receptacle for domestic use:

"But we have this treasure in jars of clay to show that this all-surpassing power is from God and not from us." (2 Corinthians 4:7)

The humility that the Buhid displayed, whilst in sharp contrast to the Westerner, also demonstrated a lack of confidence. But provided they sought the Lord, human frailty would not be a hindrance.

Finally, the last one came to the front, the youngest of all the candidates. The wind of the jeepney had evidently blown his thick hair into wild disarray, giving him an impetuous air. This was Samwil, young and stockier than the rest, his swarthy cheeks slightly reddened by the sun from riding on the roof of the jeep. He had a good-humoured face with a broad, winsome smile. Not in the least shy, he took hold of the lectern as he spoke and worked it somewhat loose in its anchoring in the earth, swaying it from one side to the other as he spoke with gusto. Sometimes he propped his whole weight against the groaning lectern and lent forward with his upper torso on top of his arms. I feared an imminent collapse.

At first, he too did not seem exactly to be champing at the bit, speaking instead of his own unworthiness. But some in the congregation had already decided he was the one and they interjected with comments and advice, which to the uninitiated onlooker appeared to win Samwil round to their way of thinking.

Samwil had deliberately been called upon last, as he was the most suitable candidate. What was taking place was a mere formality, and folk were relishing every minute of it. It was good to be together, staying up late into the night, instead of giving in to the exhaustion of the day's work. The good, bright light, the comfort of friends and family all about them, commended itself more than staying in a home lit by a poor, smokey lamp. Something of the atmosphere of a conference pervaded the place due to the gathering from many Buhid churches. Samwil was clearly enjoying it all, continuing to give the lectern further grief, carried away with the thought of going on mission.

"Don't think it will all be easy!" cautioned Danggin, a veteran missionary himself. "Not everyone is going to turn to the Lord. Not everyone is going to listen to you." Danggin paused. It seemed quite incredible how Samwil's manner had swung from self-deprecation to avid enthusiasm; his youthful swagger almost bordering on the boastful. By this time, Danggin had stood up, emphasising what he was saying. He spoke with a strident voice, quite deep, enunciating the stressed syllable in many a word. "And you know, there will even be some who will be deliberately against you because of what you are going to do! It is like fire; people will approach because it gives light and warmth, but the fire can scold and burn. Then some won't be so pleased!"

Samwil nodded vigorously and said he understood what the veteran was saying. But Samwil was young and eager to go and wanted to throw caution to the winds. It is not easy to pass on the wisdom of experience to the young and impetuous of heart. Experience is the only cure for such a one as Samwil.

This enthusiasm for mission had not come about overnight. Long before we came to Mindoro the Buhid Church had grasped their responsibility to go and tell other communities about the Almighty One who delivers from fear. Many did not need us to point out the texts that command us to go. The difference was that now they were excited about their faith. Many had met with God afresh. Others had come to know God for the very first time and their lives had been transformed by Him. Such commitment came about through teaching God's word with conviction and prayer. Many prayers had been concentrated onto these few churches and a new wind was blowing, igniting into crackling flames what had been a damp and difficult fire. Flames were appearing where before there was only smouldering.

A church cannot be renewed without the faithful preaching of the whole counsel of God's word. The truth is winsome, even when it comes from unskilled lips. Such reliance on the Spirit is more persuasive than the preacher who depends on learned skills and methods, however helpful these may be to the listener. Nothing can ever surpass the servants of the Lord, humbled by their own sense of inadequacy, overwhelmed by the magnitude of the task, who are so consumed by passion for the Lord that they get down on their knees in sheer desperation, and cry out to the Lord to soften hardened hearts and to bless those who hear His word. God delights to answer such prayers.

Next came the question of where the Buhid Church was going to commence her mission. Most of them knew that I favoured reaching out to the Bangon, a sub-tribe of the Buhid, who more or less spoke their language, but had so far not been reached with the gospel.

"Brothers and sisters!" Diokno raised his voice to gain everyone's attention and quieten the din. He waited, smiling patiently. His fine features were like the work of a master sculptor. His chiselled cheeks were illuminated in part by the pressure lamp burning close above him, yet still concealed in shadow where the contours of his face changed. He squinted in the sudden glare and turned his face slightly away from the spotlight. Now half his face was cast in shadow.

"There are several believing Buhid at Anaw," Diokno began, "some relatives of ours from Apnagan and Manihala who are asking us to send someone to teach them, as well as to evangelise the many pagan that live in the area. Do you think that we should send Samwil there?"

A thoughtful pause ensued while folk began discussing this point with their neighbour. Various people then gave their support to the proposal. I moved over to Danggin and asked him whether Samwil should be sent to the Bangon. Danggin stood up and put my concern to the assembly. I winced, as I wanted to be discreet, to avoid influencing everyone due to the credence attached to whatever the missionary said. I was just as concerned too about listening to God, open to the views of others in determining where the church's mission should begin.

It was decided there and then, however, that Samwil and his wife were to be sent to Anaw as the Buhid had a responsibility towards these few struggling believers and to the many around them who did not yet know Christ.

What had determined the Antioch church to send their missionaries first of all to Cyprus when all about them were pagan places just as needy? Undoubtedly the Holy Spirit had stirred the assembly. But was Cyprus chosen as their starting point in part because Barnabas originated from that island and so had a natural burden for its people and a knowledge of its culture? There was nothing ungodly about that. The human element is permitted to mingle with the divine in the outworking of His purposes. God chooses to operate through man.

Although disappointed it was not the Bangon, I too felt they were right to give priority to a small body of believers who were struggling so much that they were no longer meeting. The Buhid Church had a responsibility to gather them, to teach and to build them up as well as to evangelise their neighbours. I was at first surprised at how quickly they had come to this decision, not that I was questioning its validity. But then it dawned on me that again, this discussion had already been worked through beforehand and so this meeting was more to formalise the decisions. In a shorter while still, they had decided on a date to visit the few Christians in Anaw and chosen who were to go as representatives of the different churches. The meeting came to a close, surprising not only myself with its effective wrapping up of the entire matter, but others too who had come prepared for an all-night stint. Such all-night sessions were not uncommon, since the Buhid fashion of talking around the issues in decreasing concentric circles meant that reaching a consensus was often a lengthy process. I was equally pleased with the solidarity shown by the various churches present, the unanimity that the whole body felt which to me was a decisive indication that this plan was of the Lord.

* * *

"Don't come any nearer!" warned an unkempt man from within his hut, gesticulating frantically to the lone man as he approached. "Don't you know that my father has died here earlier this afternoon?"

"I know. That's why I have come to visit you and to help in whatever way I can," replied Samwil. Samwil had been in Anaw now for a few months and had come across to this unbeliever's house in an act of compassion.

"Are you not afraid? I tell you my father has died!" responded the man inside, incredulous that anyone would be so slow and foolish as not to realise the implications.

Bereavement is a very lonely time for the pagan Buhid, as everyone fears the proximity of the spirit of the deceased. The dead one, feeling lonely, may decide to strike, with a mortal bite, one of his living relatives to have their companionship in the afterlife, for the spirit, bound to a small portion of earth where the person had died, cannot wander far in search of the companionship of other spirits. Or if the deceased had a grudge and wanted to settle a score, he could inflict an illness leading to death. To avoid the spirit meddling with the living, Buhid keep a safe distance. This means that for some days following the death of a person, it is taboo to go anywhere near the hut of where they had died. Those of the same household as the deceased and neighbours in close proximity have to pass this time in isolation, until such time it is deemed safe to resume wary contact once more.

Samwil came up to the doorway of the quiet house, removed his battered rubber flip-flops and with one easy motion, launched himself up onto the doorstep, waist height from the ground. The unkempt man had withdrawn to one corner where he kneeled, stooping over the corpse. A woman was with him, busily at work with a length of rattan, weaving it in and out of the two lengths of a mat, preparing a woven coffin. The woman looked up at Samwil and then to the dishevelled man, passing the latter a curious glance before setting about her work again.

As Samwil's eyes grew accustomed to the gloom within the hut after the fierce glare of the afternoon sun, he noticed three children sitting glumly around a woven tray, picking out baked cassava with their grubby fingers. Their faces were dirty, as were their torn clothes. An air of despair hung within the hut. No one spoke. They ignored their visitor as though he was not there.

"Have you got a spade?" Samwil asked simply, wanting to be of some practical use.

There was no reply.

"Or a trenching tool will do!" continued Samwil, eyeing the inhabitants of this grim home.

The man looked up after lengthy reflection and finally said:

"There is an iron bar around the back!" Pausing, he looked Samwil boldly in the face for a moment, adding: "Are you not afraid to come here?"

"No, I have no need to be afraid," replied Samwil. "I have come to know and to follow one who has overcome death and has become my Saviour. Although the spirits of the dead have power through Satan, it is nothing compared to the power of the one who has overcome death, the one who has created you and me."

"Who is this one of whom you speak?"

"Jesus Christ. He is the one who has broken the power of the darkness and evil." Samwil paused a while to observe the effect, if any, that his words produced. The bereaved family remained impassive. "Come, let us prepare a grave and we can talk some more!"

It took a little persuasion on Samwil's part for them to accept his help, but he persisted. The two men went off together with what tools there were to select a place to dig the grave.

"Are you going to move away from here now that the old one has died?" asked Samwil, pausing to wipe his brow from the digging.

"Yes, of course," the unkempt man replied brusquely in a low voice, in fear of being overheard by the spirit of the dead or by any other spirit for that matter.

After a burial, Buhid usually abandon their homes and move a safe distance away, preferably crossing flowing water in the hope of passing beyond the area where the spirit of the dead is bound. This can mean the abandoning of several homes, should they be in close proximity to the house of the dead, then choosing a propitious time like a new moon to escape under cover of darkness in a silent conspiracy to elude the spirit of the dead. This can involve the moving of a community over the hill, across into another valley, possibly giving up former land they had worked. It entailed enquiring of others about a new place to settle, an area not linked with the passing away of the dead or any other such accursed ground. It meant having to clear the jungle and prepare new fields.

"You know, you don't need to run away!" remarked Samwil challengingly.

"How do you mean? Maybe the dead one will take one of us if we don't move quickly!" He looked at Samwil as though he was not quite in his right mind.

"Jesus, the Lord of whom I spoke earlier, is able to keep you from any such evil. Believe in Him!"

"How can I believe in one whom I don't know nor have seen?"

Samwil stabbed the iron bar into the earth, took a small red New Testament from the back pocket of his shorts and turned the well-thumbed pages. He read the following:

> "When I saw him, I fell at his feet as though dead. Then he placed his right hand on me and said: 'Do not be afraid. I am the first and the last. I am the Living One; I was dead, and behold I am alive forever and ever! And I hold the keys of death and Hades.'" (Revelation 1:17–18)

Samwil went on to explain who Jesus was, his coming into history, his death and resurrection and how all authority in heaven and earth had now been given to him. The other listened with seeming indifference as he continued about his task. But he was taking it in and mulling it all over in his mind. Samwil tapped him on the shoulder to indicate his turn to dig the deepening hole. Samwil jumped into the four-foot grave and set to with determination. The dishevelled one meanwhile scraped back the soil being thrown out, since the land was sloping and the big pile of earth needed to be retained. He then took out his fotol from its scabbard and deftly cut eight straight branches from the trees growing nearby. Having stripped them clean of all the smaller branches and twigs growing from the limb, he arranged them in layers, from the ground, one above the other, secured against two tree trunks. The soil piled up high, retained by this wall of branches.

Within the hour the grave was dug deep, deep enough for monitor lizards not to be able to smell out the corpse and dig it up. The old man was duly buried and the earth piled on top of him. Samwil detained the family a moment and prayed for them there and then to be kept from evil and harm.

Samwil then went home and the bereaved returned to their hut. They weighed in their hearts the things that Samwil had spoken about. They even talked in quiet, conspiratorial whispers of the words of this Lord Jesus. How good all of this would be if it really were true! But they were sceptical. There was no one good, no benevolent power the other side of the grave. And yet this Samwil, one of their own fellow Buhid, had expressly come to their village because he wanted them also to trust in this Lord Jesus who would free them from all their fears. They felt hope in the fearlessness Samwil showed but they needed convincing that death would not befall Samwil and his household for so blatantly breaking the taboo.

During the following days Samwil visited them regularly, urging them not to abandon home and this community. They observed, at first cautiously and then with growing conviction, that nothing bad had occurred to any of them since the old man's death. This inclined them to credit the power of the Lord Jesus.

Other pagan neighbours too were keeping a careful eye on this home as well as that of Samwil's household. They were waiting for the next illness to strike, an illness that would precede the next death. They were watching carefully and with fear, ready to take their cue at the first misadventure, to abandon home and move over the mountain. But no one fell sick in the days that followed, answering the fervent prayers of the few believers in Anaw and bringing the proof looked for by the dead man's son and his family that this Lord Jesus was indeed Lord of all, both of the living and of the dead. That following Sunday, the bereaved came along to the worship gathering, and in the Sundays that followed, more and more were added to their number, convinced of the power of Christ who could keep those who trusted in Him from the malevolence of the dead.

Through the death of one, a church came into being, the number of believers tripling within weeks until there were twenty of them. But some stubbornly would not believe, although they had seen the proof of the devil's inability to terrorise those who placed their trust in Christ. Held in a dark and dreadful grip, they felt compelled to continue in their old, hopeless ways of rampant fear, in bondage to the evil one:

> ". . . even if our gospel is veiled, it is veiled to those who are perishing. The god of this age has blinded the minds of unbelievers, so that they cannot see the light of the gospel of the glory of Christ, who is the image of God." (2 Corinthians 4:3–4)

Samwil and Ibilin and their three young children had moved to Anaw at the beginning of the year, which in the Philippines is the start of the dry season. As the Anaw community planned on moving down the hill to build a village on a new plot closer to the market where they traded, only a temporary house was built for the missionaries. As they would only be there for the duration of the dry season, a non-waterproof roof of woven palm fronds was felt adequate. However this particular year Samwil and his family had come to the village, was the year following El Niño – the time of drought that occurs at intervals around the Pacific Rim. This often produces the opposite phenomenon of La Niña, a season of heavy rains during the dry season. It rained just about every day and the woven palm fronds were quite insufficient to keep Samwil and his family dry. They spent a very miserable year, constantly wet, their bedding and spare clothes often wet or damp at the best, some even gathering mildew. They soldiered on under very trying circumstances. With the move to the new plot imminent, the construction of a more substantial roof was not considered. However the imminence of the move remained the talking point all that year, only actually taking place a year after Samwil and family had first arrived.

An inter-church team came over to Anaw during the second year of La Niña and built Samwil a proper house on the new Anaw site in just three days. During those three days the rains never abated. The temperature was uncommonly cold, perhaps dropping to around 23°C, which to northern European and US reckoning is still warm, but in the tropics is 10° lower than usual. Our church team was larger than anticipated and consequently we ran short of food and had to be content with a meagre ration of rice and nothing else to go with it except salt. One day a bottle of Bago-ong was produced, a grey, evil-smelling mixture of mashed-up, decayed fish. Everyone relished mixing a little of this in with their rice. For once I was well content to make do with just the salt as my rice accompaniment!

The hard-working party was not being fed enough to keep warm. The 20 or so of us huddled together for warmth at night on the floor of one room which had two walls yet to be built. The nights brought blustery squalls of rain sweeping through the house at the very angle where the walls were missing, periodically waking us all. Everyone stayed remarkably good humoured, even the six who had to sleep outside stretched out on sawn planks under an extended eave but without a wall screen to shelter behind. They were wetter and colder than anyone. I admired their tenacity and readiness to be thankful for every small mercy. Their joy of being together about a common purpose, serving the Lord in a very practical way, was exemplary.

The work party, keen to have communal devotions, asked me to lead them. The first one was fixed straight after breakfast, another one before lunch and the third after the evening meal. Together we studied the letters to the seven churches at the beginning of Revelation. We were particularly impressed by the Lord Jesus' deeply perceptive view of the condition of each church, often quite contrary to external appearances. To think of how Jesus would view the various churches represented there in this inter-church work party was sobering, causing us to consider Christ's view of our churches. It inspired the leaders not to become complacent, or satisfied by the status quo, recognising that self-satisfaction can be very deluding, blinding us to our real state and need.

Much of the Western Church can be highly selective in choosing scripture which encourages and affirms the individual and tends rather to ignore, or brush over the warnings of becoming complacent. We do so at our own peril, heedless that we limit our view of God who judges the believer. Ignoring the piercing gaze of Christ will tend to keep us spiritual dwarves, reared on an inoculation of God's goodness and grace to protect us from the hostile world about us.

Is there not a lack of thirsting after God's righteousness, of wanting to go deeper into the Christian life to allow our faith to take us beyond our comfort zone? By limiting our discipleship, we are forsaking the blessing of God's grace, who enables us to grow and to move on. By denying God access into the no-go areas in our lives, we deny ourselves the greater reality of knowing God more intimately.

My lasting impression of those stormy days was an image of Samwil crouching down on his haunches up on the raised floor of the house under construction, holding on to one of the supporting posts, disconsolately looking down at the rain-splattered mud. I did not know at the time, nor did anyone else I believe, that Samwil was having second thoughts about continuing here at Anaw. The season of rain had taken its toll on that young family. Furthermore, with another baby on its way, Samwil was counting the cost again. He observed the rising prosperity of his fellow men back in Apnagan whilst he had to make do with the relatively meagre provision the churches could afford to give him.

His heart was no longer in the work.

We left Anaw and a house almost complete save for a few minor details. Samwil never went back.

CHAPTER NINE

A HOME IN MANIHALA

Deborah was out alone on the hillside, gathering wood before making the two-mile journey back home. She had already unearthed and filled a basket full of sweet potatoes and trimmed off a couple of bundles of their green tops from their field. These tops she planned to cook into a watery stew flavoured with ginger root.

A movement over in the bushes made her look up – perhaps it was a water buffalo taking advantage of the shade in the sultry afternoon.

She was shocked to see a Luktanon, totally naked, looking straight at her. Averting her eyes she turned about to make for home. In her confusion, the direction she took was not towards her village. Aware of her vulnerability in that lonely place, her one thought was to escape quickly but calmly. As she walked briskly away, she heard a sudden twanging noise, just once, like that made by a taut bowstring being released. On hearing that unexpected sound, she instantly felt a searing pain in her side, like something sharp piercing her flesh, as far as to her spleen. The pain was so excruciating that she had to stop. She released the bark band from her forehead that secured the basket to her back, carelessly letting it fall heavily to the ground. The sweet potatoes scattered down the slope. She fell to her knees, doubled up with the agony in her side. Fearing what might happen next she turned awkwardly to see if the naked man was coming towards her.

No one was there. The bushes where she had seen him a moment before were motionless, seeming to swoon in the hot afternoon sun. All was quite still. Even the fronds of the coconut palm were not stirring.

Suddenly Deborah vomited with the intensity of the pain. This brought no relief; the retching only further induced more suffering. When she removed her hand, which all this time had been clutching her side, to examine the wound, she noticed it was quite bloodless! She felt something long, thin and sharp had pierced her side, like an arrow. She recalled again hearing the bowstring.

There was a total absence of blood emerging from the wound. She looked at her T-shirt stained with many things, but blood, fresh blood, was not one of the stains. She pulled up her shirt to look at the flesh itself and was astonished to see no mark. Yet the pain was real.

Again she vomited, this time only bile.

"O Lord Jesus," she cried out, "help me! Deliver me from this pain!"

The pain subdued somewhat and the vomiting ceased. There was no sign of the naked man.

Ready to take up her basket once more, she gathered up the scattered contents and, picking up a small pile of firewood, she went towards home, not caring that she had not collected enough wood.

She feared the naked man might still be around, preparing to do her more harm. She needed to move now, whilst the pain had abated somewhat, for if it intensified again, how would she reach home?

"Oy – Deborah, what is troubling you?" an old woman's voice called out from a ramshackle house as Deborah came into her village of Manihala half an hour later. Deborah looked on over to the open doorway of the nearby house, but could see no one there. She stumbled on, fearing she was hearing voices now. She did not even take note whose house it was.

Again the voice called out to her. It was her grandmother's, she realised then, and recognising that familiar voice brought great consolation. She looked back to the open doorway where the bright sunshine fell on the threshold, accentuating the darkness within, and there her elderly grandmother crawled into view. She beckoned to Deborah, fixing her with her one good eye, scrutinising her closely, for her other eye had turned milky with a cataract. Deborah went over and told her grandmother what had happened.

The house was greatly dilapidated and would have been abandoned by a younger person a good year ago. She was full of years and not expected to live much longer. Her sons did not think it worth their while to build her a new home, but rather patched it up, securing large leaves under the roof slats where there was a leak. Her home was joined to that of her eldest son at the roof, his house being only slightly better maintained. The grass roof inside was not only black from woodsmoke, but had been so well fumigated over the years that a shiny coat of tar gave it a lustrous appearance. The room was largely bare except for a couple of blackened cooking pots and a large field basket. The basket was now used for storing clothes and a blanket made up from sewn-up rice sacks.

"It was an evil spirit you saw who shot you with a dart!" declared the grandmother in a thin voice. "In the old days when this happened, you went to the one who had the ability to massage the dart out from under your skin. My uncle had that secret knowledge and could bring relief. He would just work his fingers around where the dart had entered, push his fingers deep into the abdomen until he could feel the dart and strangely was able to pluck it out. You could see the dart in his hand that he had taken from within. But that is not our way now, is it?"

The elderly woman had been preparing a chew of betel nut all this time whilst she was telling Deborah the account she had told many times before. She placed a portion of a large snail's shell into a short bamboo section and pounded it with a thin iron rod bent at right angles near the point. This provided the essential ingredient of lime. Taking out a leaf from her woven bag, she put the betel nut onto the leaf and with a sprinkling of ground lime from the bamboo container, wrapped it all up into a neat parcel and popped it into her mouth with evident relish. The mixture immediately stimulated the saliva glands. She closed her eyes in abandonment and chewed with toothless gums on the package. Her face was dirty with fire ash from having slept too close to the hearth, something that she did at nights since she no longer had a husband to sidle up to in the cold. Her clothes were very ragged and of one colour, grey from banana sap and ash. Deborah looked at her, indifferent to this picture of poverty, thinking how helpful it was to have told someone, to have her own suspicions confirmed that the naked person had been no ordinary man.

The pain in her side still bothered her, but no longer with the former intensity that had induced her to vomit. She took out some sweet potatoes from her large basket, removed some of the green tops from the bundle and, placing these down beside her grandmother's withered thigh, said that she was going. The grandmother did not move but lay there on her broken floor where the bamboo slats had snapped in places and had come loose from their vine bindings. She leant her back against a wall prop, intently chewing with eyes closed, motionless except for her jaw working steadily away. Totally preoccupied in extracting the most from her chew, she did not acknowledge her departing granddaughter.

Over the coming days, Deborah's abdomen swelled and the skin turned red, hot to the touch. The rest she had taken from the field work had not brought the recovery hoped for, and her husband – Gano – had already decided it was time to take her down to the lowlands to see a doctor, especially since a fever had started. They set off early one morning after breakfast, Gano placing his wife on horseback and beginning the steep descent with two of their sons. The eldest one came only to return with the horse once they reached the road at the bottom. He was to keep an eye on things and to take their water buffalo twice daily to the river. The youngest son they left with one of Deborah's sisters.

The doctor down in their nearby town of Bansud said Deborah had an internal growth that maybe was cancerous and advised an operation that could only be done at Calapan. Gano was to take his wife there as soon as possible in the ambulance. Gano shook his head on hearing how much the ambulance would cost. He did not have enough money to cover it. Besides, the money that he had brought along would be needed to pay for the doctor's consultation, for medicines and for their food. He feared that the little he had would soon run out.

Gano had a very friendly and charming appearance, and whether it was this, or the Lord's prompting, the outcome was regarded by them as providential. The doctor said the ambulance would take them free of charge all the way to Calapan. They had never travelled by ambulance before, a vehicle running so much more smoothly than the jeepneys and buses. For their son, this was an exciting adventure that made him forget the reason for their travelling in such style. Gano specifically prayed that Deborah would not need an operation, as everyone feared surgery for the appalling reputation it had out in the provinces, where so many never recovered even from relatively simple operations. Surgery was very much regarded as the final straw.

The doctor in Calapan was a young man who wanted to know exactly how this internal wound, now so terribly infected, had been inflicted. Deborah rather sheepishly told the intelligent young doctor about the naked man and the sound of the bowstring. She had wanted to leave that detail out but felt an inner compulsion not to.

"I don't think that we need to operate," the doctor announced much to Gano's visible relief. "Tell me, are you Christians?"

The couple vigorously nodded their heads.

"I am too!" continued the doctor. "Well, I tell you what we are going to do. We are going to pray, because I very much suspect prayer is the only thing that is going to help you as this is not a normal condition but one caused by the devil."

The young doctor closed his eyes and, placing his hand lightly on Deborah's swollen abdomen, he led in a prayer of healing, simple and short, but full of trust in God's ability to undo this appalling work. He was fairly sure of his own diagnostic hunch.

Within the hour, the fever and the swelling had totally gone and they were discharged from the hospital. Not only had the Lord swiftly answered the doctor's prayer, but Gano's earlier prayer too when he had asked God to spare his wife from having an operation. God had guided the couple to Calapan where they could be helped by a doctor's spiritual insight.

We heard all about this from Deborah and Gano next time we stayed in their village of Manihala. On this follow-up visit, they were hosting us again in their house perched on a steep hillside with a breathtaking view below of the tropical coast and the South China Sea. Deborah was one of the keenest Christians in Manihala, running the children's Sunday school single-handed. It surprised us that Satan could inflict such a wound on one of the more mature Christians. It was usually the immature and the unbelieving whom Satan could wound in this manner, victims who had given him a foothold, ones unsure of their faith.

Alexandra produced from her backpack a large bundle of new books and bulky envelopes filled with drawings and photocopies, a package that all Sunday schools were being equipped with, funded by the Sunday school of our home church. We were thankful for how far their gift had stretched, forming a tangible link between these churches of the "highlanders" (the meaning of the word "Buhid") of Mindoro, with our church in the Scottish Highlands. Deborah thumbed through these brand new materials with wonder and delight, whilst I sat with Gano in the far corner of their house, teaching him how to read. Alexandra went through the basic explanation of how the lessons were structured, something which the Buhid were asking for as they had a problem retaining the children's attention, leading to threats of discipline. They admitted that this was not a desirable environment if they were to encourage the children to continue coming to these sessions.

The lesson plan was simple. A Bible story was told in the teacher's own words, employing all the dynamics of story-telling, followed by emphasising the main spiritual point, a memory verse, and a game or drama based on the spiritual principle or Bible story. For them the *pièce de résistance* was a line drawing for the children to colour in, with the memory verse underneath and the relevant Bible passage written out in full on the reverse. This proved so popular in all the villages that often the children had to make way for their parents who had never had anything like this! The children were ecstatic over the coloured wax crayons that were part of this pack.

The following afternoon, Deborah called together a few of her sisters and others who could become future helpers in this work. A crowd of children also eagerly gathered in the church. Alexandra demonstrated what was meant by telling an interesting story, using action, mime and inflecting her voice. The women giggled and at times stifled laughter in their wide-open-mouthed delight at how a Bible story could be told. The moment of horror came though to these shy ladies when Alexandra delegated different Bible stories to each of them to retell. Some of them struggled far less than expected, showing natural ability in storytelling. Their efforts would have been better still had we, their missionaries, not been standing by listening to them.

What commended this teaching package to them was its variety, and how different gifts were needed for the various parts. Those who were not such natural storytellers were often good at organising a game or a drama.

When we first came to the Manihala church, Gano was the main elder. Being totally illiterate, only able to read and write his own name, he did the best he could in retelling the Bible stories he had heard. His father-in-law – Bagaw – usually the main elder, had been trained at the Bible school. But now this senior figure was pre-occupied with local politics to such a degree that he had to be absent from the church much of the time and was unaware of what was going on.

Gano and the other inexperienced elders responded warmly to an offer from the Iglesia ni Cristo (meaning the "Church of Christ") cult, who, having a building down the hillside, had proposed to teach them properly in the faith. The problem was, despite the encouraging-sounding name of the church, they taught that Christ was a man only. This cult had been started 70 years before by a Filipino and had now grown to fantastic proportions within the Philippines and was even spreading abroad through migrant Filipino workers. The cult had just finished a week-long seminar to indoctrinate the Buhid Christians in their homespun falsehood. The Buhid had all the leaflets and tracts to show and were surprised at my condemnation of their teaching. They asked me why this doctrine was wrong. Did they not also teach about God and His chosen Christ?

I had, without ulterior motive, planned to do a short series of teaching through the first two chapters of John's gospel. This was ideal in addressing the issue of the divine nature of Christ. Having arrived late on the previous day from Apnagan, I was a little apprehensive preaching there for the first time. Just as I was getting into full swing in my exposition of the first twelve verses of John's gospel, Bagaw, Gano's father-in-law, rose to his feet and, facing the whole congregation from the front, exclaimed with passion:

"Brothers and sisters, hear what the scriptures say about our Lord Jesus. He is the Lord God there at the beginning of the world through whom all things were made. Our missionary teaches true, listen to him and take note and you will realise why those Iglesia ni Cristo people are wrong!" He smiled at me with a mixture of apology and passion and sat down. He beckoned me to continue.

I enjoyed this spontaneous response from the congregation in the middle of preaching a sermon. It was especially appreciated at that moment, for until then I had been unaware of the gravity of the situation. New to the area, it encouraged me greatly to have the blessing of this leader, however distant he may have grown from the church. Again this was God's providence that this busy man – Bagaw – should be there in church that Sunday.

Preaching back in Scotland, I discovered, was a far more uncertain matter, since I could never be sure if I was communicating or not. Our minister back in Scotland sometimes chides his listeners, saying it is all right to nod our heads, as long as we are in agreement! In the Mangyan churches there was often much head nodding, the very minimum response from a congregation. I was surprised the first time when an old fellow interrupted me in midflow during a sermon and reiterated a point I had made, just to be sure that he had understood it correctly. Following the first interruption, I was never again surprised and enjoyed the responsiveness as a sign that they considered the teaching important. Likewise questions would be occasionally asked or a cultural anecdote made as a helpful application, making it a learning session for myself as well.

In fact it came to the point when I considered I had not properly communicated, or my presentation had been lacklustre, when there were no interruptions. The Buhid were also adept at reading my mood, knowing when it was not appropriate to interrupt. The majority of questions were normally reserved until after we had covered the teaching material for that session, and these would be numerous, particularly on the last night of my stay in a place. Then they found an extra boldness, wanting to make the most of the last opportunity there would be for a long while, to ask, one question stimulating another, and often the sessions went on into the early hours of the morning.

During our field trip to Ayan Bekeg, it had been brought to our attention that the Mormons were targeting the weak churches and how those churches had resisted. Those fragile churches had said they only knew of the Bible as being God's word, and on the strength of that, had declined the Mormons' invitation to be led into fuller truth! Here in Manihala was a duplicate situation, a weak church being led by men quite unequal to the task. The members of the Iglesia ni Cristo were trained in the art of debate, and like many of the cults, could recite many texts in support of their particular views, to dumbfound the not-so-very-certain and make them wonder, why before then, they had not really found the truth! Maybe this cult had the answer, the Buhid reasoned, maybe they were God's appointed agents at this time of need, to lead them deeper in knowing God more intimately.

In providence, we arrived in Manihala at that crucial time when they were deciding whether to join up with that church down the mountainside. God had equipped us with a message so appropriate to the issue at stake – the deity of Christ.

As I taught Gano how to read and write, I soon found that a large portion of the young adult population were at best only semi-literate. Therefore I ran literacy classes for the best part of the community in the church. Their inability to read and search the scriptures for themselves contributed greatly to their ignorance of these basic doctrines.

One trip when we went up to Manihala, Gano led us as usual to his house. As it was almost dusk and we were tired from the journey and the climb, we had not noticed anything different. Nor had Gano said anything to us. But instead of going into his home, he stood at his house corner and catching our attention said, "This is yours!" He beckoned to a new house built beside his own. We were quite overwhelmed for he had not even given us the slightest inkling of building us a house! His father-in-law confided that it had been entirely Gano's idea and he had built it all himself.

What particularly touched me about the house was that he had positioned it right in front of his living room window where often I sat to admire the fantastic view of the coast. The following morning, having taught and eaten breakfast, we sat at our own window. The open panorama took in the South China Seas stretching as far as the eye could see, to distant islands dotted with palms. As we drank in the astounding beauty of the scene, our gaze came in to focus on one spot where the sea burst into a pale green, rimmed with white, where it was breaking on an offshore coral reef. A bold, grassy hill rose in the mid-foreground, the flanks of which, bristling with banana groves, presented a slope of stirring green. The fierce glare of tropical light reflecting off the shiny surfaces of the banana fronds, produced a shimmering haze-like quality to the hillside, as though it too were sailing ever so slowly upon the South China Seas. The occasional flame tree reared above the banana groves, with flashes of huge orange blossoms, added as though by an artist's whim, with extravagant dabbing of a brush on an exotic canvas. On either side of this luxuriant hill, Mindoro's shore formed a long bow, a 20-mile arch that we could see from our hill, terminating in a peninsula at one end, and lost in a blur at the other in the mangrove swamps beyond Bongabong.

Gano had obliterated the view from his own home, a view he too greatly admired, instead gifting it to us. What generosity! We could only enjoy this view for nine days in every three months when we visited Manihala. Gano had a big heart and this unsolicited gift drew us close together. Gano and Deborah still insisted on doing all the cooking, stressing that we were to eat at their house, leaving us free to teach and pastor.

That same month, another house was built for us in Apnagan, again totally out of the blue. These incredibly generous gestures, more than anything else, told us we were welcome. We had become part of their tribal community. We were considered "fellow Buhid" as they frequently informed other Buhid who did not know us and the Mangyan of other tribes.

*   *   *

Soon after that visit to Manihala, I had been on my way to Siyangi, but owing to a succession of setbacks, I had missed the first jeepney.

When I boarded the next trip, a couple of hours later, we had a puncture midway and with the spare tyre being damaged too, the driver had no recourse other than to wait for a tricycle – which passed most infrequently along that lonely hill road – to take the wheel to be repaired. The driver took the best part of two hours to return from town with the repaired tyre and so by the time I arrived at the bridge at Lisap, I was at least four hours later than usual. What was more, the recently repaired bridge was down again. The final span was a tangled piece of metal debris trailing limp from the road level, disturbing the swift current of the river below. My first thought was that this was an act of sabotage. However, an overloaded cargo jeepney, in spite of the local warnings, had proceeded onto the lightweight bridge and brought it down.

The party coming from Siyangi to meet me had returned home disappointed. The Siyangi trail was more dangerous for me to travel on alone than some others, and I was not going to risk it without companions. More than once I had been threatened with a beating by Luktanon who lived beside the Siyangi trail, for their son had been imprisoned for murdering a Buhid. They threatened revenge on me, for the Hanselmans had reported this murder to the police. The Luktanon family insisted that I was the Hanselmans' son. I was therefore faced with the choice of either returning home to Bongabong, or proceeding to nearby Batangan.

These circumstances had conspired to direct me to Batangan instead. Upon my arrival, one of the elderly believers hastened to tell me that Christa was not at all well.

Whilst Christa had had no more intimidating experiences from the powers of darkness, she had been obviously scarred by the experience and was far from right. Her spine had suffered injury when she had hurled herself from a height when under the tyrannical influence of the demons, and since then she had physically suffered considerably. The vitamins and iron tablets we had given her when she became pregnant had been left untouched. She had not liked the taste and so had decided not to continue taking them!

I visited Christa and was shocked by her degraded state. The house was filled with the foul odour of someone who had not washed for ages. She was curled up asleep in the middle of the floor with her child sitting up pathetically beside her. The child's filthy face was streaked by recent tears, cleaning away some of the thickly accumulated grime. Her eyes bulged in her oversized-looking head, a sight common among the malnourished. The eighteen-month-old child was now too weak and forlorn to bother crying more, for all her protests had been ignored. I was struck by the pointed pro-tuberances of Christa's skeletal form even showing through from under a blanket grey with filth. Part of an arm and a leg lay exposed beyond the blanket's cover, totally emaciated, lying slackly against the thin strips of bamboo flooring. The limbs were just wrinkled skin upon bone. This was a picture entitled "Waiting for Death".

Christa's mother returned with water flagons at that moment and despite my protests, woke Christa up in that usual brusque manner the Mangyan have with one another, not having the same respect others have for the sick who are sleeping. It had been over three months since I last saw Christa. Back then, she and her husband were still attending church. Two years had passed since she had been delivered from the terrifying ordeals of those demonic visitors she used to encounter on her way to church. Now Christa looked like one who had given up the will to live. She reminded me of an injured bird who had abandoned all hope, lying there resigned, waiting for those brief, pathetic death throes. The mother told me that for quite a while now, Christa had not left the house.

I challenged this eighteen-year-old mother as to whether she wanted to get better again? She nodded her head, but I did not believe that mild assent. Having heard the hopeless saga of her going downhill and of her husband's frequent prolonged absences from the home, it was apparent Christa and her family had given up all hope of her pulling through. I led them in prayer, asking for the Lord to intervene. I admit to not having had the faith to ask God to heal her, for I felt the sick had a moral part to play in healing by at least wanting to be made whole again.

Early in the evening of that same day, I returned with Monay and his wife Talad to anoint her with oil, and again we prayed for her. Christa was more responsive and put herself right with the Lord. That evening, Monay shared in church how he had especially sensed the presence of God at Christa's house, and we wondered how all this would work out in view of Monay's faith coupled with my unexpected arrival in Batangan. It seemed that God had orchestrated our being together at this anxious time in the lives of Christa and her family.

I left the following day in a second, successful attempt to reach Siyangi. There too, I met with a church much subdued, mourning the death of a 40-year-old mother and somebody's toddler. Sickness was rife and all sorts of reports abounded of mass rebel movements in the vicinity. It was rumoured that rebels were planning a massive lightning strike at places throughout Mindoro on the lowland police, army and town halls. In the midst of all the gloom and doom, there were the bright rays of hope, for the gospel had penetrated into far-flung places in the central mountains, among a people formerly resistant to the message of hope. All these things, coupled with the damaged bridge at Lisap, the fast approach of the year 2000, the mysterious characters written across the flanks of Mount Sumagui after a landslide cleared sections of mahogany forest, the fall of meteor showers, suggested to the elderly believers that the end times were here, for these things were perhaps harbingers of apocalyptic doom. These signs filled them more with foreboding than with anticipation of the Lord's return.

I abandoned my prepared programme of teaching and took up the theme of counteracting evil times with faith, as exemplified by the lives of some of the Bible saints such as Jehoshaphat and Hezekiah, Paul and John.

CHAPTER TEN

THE SUPREMACY OF CHRIST

"I'm coming with you!" called out Awang, sprinting up the slope from his brother's house to join us on the trail from Manihala back down to the road at the base of the mountains. He wiped a grain of rice from his mouth whilst still chewing on the last of his breakfast.

There were already four Buhid accompanying us on the trail, so Awang's presence was not due to protocol. Nevertheless he sought our company, having something on his mind he wanted to share. His face was beaming like that of a young lad allowed to go to town for the very first time, full of eager anticipation.

Staying at his brother's house, Awang had been full of wisecracks at the start of the seminar nine days earlier and generally made light of our topic of Christ's victory over the powers of darkness. His presence proved quite a strain, leading us to pray specifically for him. How the Lord had answered prayer, because during the course of the ensuing days, he came under the ancient power of the word of God. The kind of person of whom teachers are quite understandably wary, Awang's questions would make light of, or divert attention from, the topic rather than being the product of some heart-searching.

Awang struck me as a very worldly type of man, out to profit, making the most of every situation to promote his own cause and reputation. He was the elected representative of the Buhid in the Bansud municipal district, directly under the employment of the district mayor. I suspect he first came to the teaching sessions out of some misplaced hope of extorting some money either from us or the mission, or at least gain a financial promise to help fund one of his projects. Awang was out to further his prestige as the local leader of the Anaw community, two mountain ridges over to the north from Manihala. But God had brought him over to Manihala because there was something Awang had to hear.

> "For the word of God is living and active. Sharper than any double-edged sword, it penetrates even to dividing soul and spirit, joints and marrow; it judges the thoughts and attitudes of the heart. Nothing in all creation is hidden from God's sight. Everything is uncovered and laid bare before the eyes of him to whom we must give account." (Hebrews 4:12–13)

The Bible addressed issues in Awang's life, cutting through the worldly ambition and the political intrigue, reaching the very core of this man to lay bare his soul. After nine days of Bible study and worship, Awang was changed. All trail long, he plied me with questions about the things we had studied, anxious to clarify each matter whilst the issue was sharp in his mind, and before he would lose the opportunity of addressing these things personally to me. He opened up about his own spiritual pilgrimage which had not just commenced during the course of the last nine days, but had begun much earlier, even before he had married. Awang, like his brother Bagaw, had grown up in the Manihala church. Whilst Bagaw went on and grew in the Lord, making his way through Bible school and on to lead the Manihala church for a time, Awang seemed to go off the boil, finding his niche in a political career, whilst still involved, as all Buhid are, in the day-to-day running of his land.

He had had the opportunity of a fresh start by the coming of the Buhid missionary couple, Samwil and Ibilin, to his village. It was revealing that this man, who undoubtedly had leadership ability and the mental capacity, should have done nothing about gathering the church before the time Samwil had come to Anaw; such was the low state of his spiritual life. Following Samwil's arrival, Awang seemed to attend the meetings regularly, but had been criticised by others in the church who said that by the power of Satan, and not by God, the sick became well again when he prayed for them. Awang was hurt by their attitude. I understood from others that he was in a power conflict with another man in the church, besides Samwil, to be recognised as the leader. Whatever the truth, Awang had appeared to be promoting his own ambitions and I spoke frankly to him about that. I warned him too of the risk of any of us being used by the enemy to disrupt the church, if we did not humble ourselves first and submit to God.

This seminar topic had struck home with many like Awang. Sometimes teaching does not always relate to daily issues, and the concerns of the individual, and so becomes detached from the practical and necessary. I suspect that much of my earlier teaching was like that, that however biblically sound it might have been, it just did not connect with reality, with people's needs.

Several elders, like Monay and Diokno, suggested I tackle the issue concerning demonic intimidation and the growing observance of superstitions and taboos. These powers of darkness had been distinctly reasserting themselves from the very time the churches were waking up and showing renewed interest in God. Instances of Christians being traumatised were not just limited to

"This is yours!" Gano beckoned us to a new house in Manihala, here being enjoyed by Hannah and Iain.

Alexandra cooking in our kitchen at Siyangi.

*Inggoy, the blacksmith. How like fashioning a fotol,
using fire and hammer, is the making of a man of God.*

It was a pleasure to equip and train Sunday schools.

*Martin on the doorstep of our Siyangi home,
preparing for a teaching session.*

*Alexandra helping prepare Sunday school lessons with
two teachers in our kitchen at Apnagan.*

Zegmay, our neighbour's daughter, cooks breakfast.
Families halve coconuts and dry them for copra above the fire.

Barefoot in the mud, the Buhid gather bananas, their cash crop.

Baptism often expresses a readiness to face a test of faith.

Alexandra doing the laundry in the Madling River, Batangan.

Samwil working at Anaw, perhaps having second thoughts about the cost of mission.

Anaw brought home by bullock cart to Siyangi after an operation. At the front is Sulmay who was destined to lead the new church at Baliya Fontan.

*Alexandra reads the Buhid New Testament
to a blind neighbour in Apnagan.*

The high stilt houses of Siyangi.

Smoking a mango tree.
(Photo: John Richards)

Deborah and the demonic bowman, or to Christa, but to many others also. It had taken me two years of living with the Buhid before I began to teach about the secure position of the believer in Christ. I had been aware of the need for such teaching for a while, but I had needed to research and prepare my teaching materials and this had taken much longer than expected. The delay was perhaps indicative also of the ploys of the adversary to divert me to other topics. Much would probably have been gained sooner, had I dealt with this issue earlier. This basic need for assurance was the immediate need of all Buhid, without which all other teaching was premature and only of partial benefit. This was basic evangelism, the foundation upon which to build everything else, and it had taken me over two years to realise this fundamental starting point!

I had already run this seminar once previously at Apnagan, explaining the power of Christ over the satanic system, and had been impressed by the huge turnout. Normally teaching sessions over the Friday and Saturday nights would draw a large crowd, but come the other nights of the week, the turnout would be limited to the very keen, which in Apnagan still amounted to a significant number of people. However there was no such fluctuation in attendance throughout the seminar in Apnagan, the church remained full with many taking notes and asking questions, referring much of what they heard to their personal experiences. Here, finally, was much-needed teaching, concerning the very issue in so many Christians' lives. Finally the itch had been found where I could scratch and bring relief.

One magnificent evening, as I sat upon a ridge top watching the remaining embers of the sunset fade away behind the lofty mountain ridge to the west, I witnessed the following domestic scene outside Gano's house, a little way below me.

"'Smail – come on in immediately!" The obvious alarm in Deborah's tone indicated to the eleven-year-old lad coming up the slope to the house that he was not to dally. Ismail responded at once, bounding up the steep hillside as though competing in a race and was across the threshold of the house in no time at all.

Whilst watching this scene, I heard a coarse cackle, a haunting staccato bird-like noise, "kaw-kaw-kaw", grow louder, pass overhead, and then diminish as it flew over the banana groves beyond the house. It was growing dark and, not having brought my torch, I decided it was time too to head for home. As I approached their house, I had a strong impulse to pay them a quick call, quite contrary to my usual practice of going into my own house adjacent to theirs.

The fire was burning brightly under the two cooking pots just inside, close to the entrance. As no one was tending them, I coughed to announce my presence. Deborah's face peered anxiously round the inner door and, seeing my familiar face, she smiled and beckoned me to ascend onto the raised floor of their living quarters. Being on my own, before going into the house I asked whether Gano, her husband, was home, for I made it a rule never to enter a house on my own when the husband was not present. She called out her husband's name, announcing I was there.

I climbed up onto the slightly springy bamboo floor, carefully treading to avoid the weak and broken parts where I knew them to be, doubting that these would bear my greater weight. Gano rose from his corner, where he had been seated in a tight huddle with his children. He took hold of an old shirt and wiped clean a place on the floor for me to sit. Not aware of it being dirty, this action seemed to be done more as a gesture of welcome.

I asked after the cut on their youngest son's foot that had become swollen with infection. Deborah took up the guttering oil lamp and tipped it on its side to wet the rag wick. The room grew brighter as the flame doubled in size, and a slender, sooty plume of thick black smoke rose into the darkness. She placed the lamp close to the boy's foot so that I could inspect it. The three-year-old moaned as his mother took hold of his injured foot. I advised her to put hot compresses on the inflammation to draw off the pus, adding that we should pray for the wound to heal soon. Before praying, I asked if there were other health matters or concerns they would like prayer for. Deborah paused. Her laugh revealed there to be something, but she was unsure whether to share it. She looked to Gano for confirmation before proceeding.

"Pray for 'Smail too that he would remain strong . . ."

I probed a little as to what concern they might have.

"You can never be too sure. Just earlier he was late in coming indoors and an aswang flew right overhead just as he reached the door!" (The aswang are powerful spirit beings, half-man, half-bird in appearance.)

"You see," continued Gano, who had been quiet up until that time, "maybe the aswang managed to bite him before he got inside." The son sidled up to his father, looking frightened.

"It is right to be mindful of the enemy," I responded. "But remember he is not the all-powerful one. We have the Lord in whom we can trust." I scratched my head thoughtfully. "Just think too – I was outside at the same time that 'Smail was out and I haven't run home in a panic!"

They laughed to pass off their embarrassment. "Do you remember our teaching last night about what Jesus said before he was taken up into heaven?" I paused whilst they unsuccessfully tried to recall what he had said. "'All authority in heaven and on earth has been given to me,' Jesus had said, for the devil had been defeated by the cross and the resurrection." I then asked them for a Bible and drew their attention to Ephesians 1:18 which I asked Gano to read.

"'I pray also that the eyes of your heart may be enlightened in order that you may know the hope to which he has called you, the riches of his glorious inheritance in the saints, and his incomparably great power for us who believe,'" Gano read slowly with great deliberation.

"Is there a power greater than that of God?" I asked them. They affirmed there was not. "And what is it Paul asks for in this prayer that might be done for the Ephesian believers?" They re-read the passage again and after brief reflection, tentatively replied that Paul prayed they would truly believe.

"Are you showing faith by sitting here afraid of the aswang?"

"No!" asserted Gano. "We should pray and trust in God's greater power!" He asked one of his sons for a pen. Receiving the pen, he clumsily underlined the verses he had read.

"Since you like what you read, go on and read the very last two verses of that chapter."

"'And God placed all things under his feet and appointed him to be head over everything for the Church, which is his body, the fullness of him who fills everything in every way,'" Gano read, nodding his head in agreement with the dawning truth. It was not the first time he had read these verses, but only now was their significance becoming clear. Christ had received authority to subdue all powers and to rule. His enemies were already under His conquering feet, a picture of decisive triumph.

"And who is the Church?" I went on.

"We are, I suppose," replied the couple after a moment's hesitation and a conferring look at one another.

"Yes, we are that body with Christ as our head, whose power fills us if only we would truly believe."

We prayed together and I detected a note of new-found confidence as they spoke to their Lord. The completeness of Christ's victory withdrew the doubt and fear that had blinded them all this time. Had it been this uncertainty and fear that had made Deborah vulnerable to the spirit bowman?

Many were being defeated every time they went running indoors on hearing what they assumed to be an aswang taking flight over their homes at dusk. Mature Buhid Christians say there is a bird that makes the call the aswang is supposed to make, the raucous "kaw-kaw-kaw" sound, as it takes flight at dusk. Therefore most of these fearful experiences were nothing more than a bird taking flight. But bird or not, it is still defeat for a Christian to run from what he believes to be a demon. The Bible is not quiet about the demonic and provides examples of men of faith who overcame the forces of darkness. This is nowhere more clearly exemplified than in the life of Christ as He cast out demons from those possessed, an ability that is the birthright of His disciples. Note that when the

72 returned, whom Jesus had sent out to announce the Kingdom of God to be near, they returned with joy and said:

> "'Lord, even the demons submit to us in your name.'
> He replied, 'I saw Satan fall like lightning from heaven. I have given you authority to trample on snakes and scorpions and to overcome all the power of the enemy; nothing will harm you. However, do not rejoice that the spirits submit to you, but rejoice that your names are written in heaven.'" (Luke 10:17–18)

Far from being fearful of devilish phenomena, Jesus' followers were bold and had probably reached the point of being perhaps over-confident and triumphalistic, as suggested by Jesus' warning to focus their joy on their salvation rather than on the realised power over the realm of evil. How different were the Buhid who needed to be liberated from their centuries-long fear.

The turnout to the seminar in Manihala was just as impressive as in Apnagan, although Manihala was under half the size in population and more immature as a church. Men and women who were not in the habit of coming to church other than on a Sunday morning, were now attending, word having gone round about how life-changing the studies were.

With the bright illumination from a Tilley lamp, we were able to continue our studies way into the night. Until this visit, those in Manihala had not been keen to come out after dark. Formerly we used to have a late-afternoon session, working through the first thirteen chapters of Acts, performing a drama, chapter by chapter, to help the details and events be not only better understood, but to allow the Buhid to put themselves in the position of the early believers. These dramas were followed up with a quiz, the correct answers plotting the teams' progress on the chalkboard by colouring in another stage of Paul's journey on a ready-drawn map. The dramas were enjoyed by all, old and young, believers and sceptics alike, filling the church with a happy and expectant throng as they waited to see their child or aunt perform their part.

The seminar topic, the believer's position in Christ's victory over the powers of darkness, was an innovation here. It required serious study and sustained concentration. I wondered how the Manihala Christians were going to cope under the unusual pressure of such study.

We met opposition and perhaps some would accuse me of over-spiritualising these circumstances. We encountered significant problems with the new pressure lamp, for it would fade all of a sudden before going out, and many were genuinely afraid when the lamp was extinguished in this manner. Much courage had been required on their part to venture out of doors in the dark, fearing the aswang as they did, especially considering the distance some of them came from homes that were scattered along the hill ridge. For the new lamp to behave like this played further on their already heightened sense of fear and dread. For many, this was an omen that they really should have stayed at home. I recall getting them all to start singing hymns to focus their minds on the Lord, whilst I fiddled with the lamp. Although I am not a technical man, I had used these pressure lanterns in all of the churches and was somewhat used to their quirks and idiosyncrasies. I generally found them fairly straightforward to fix, all except for this new one in Manihala that played up for no accountable reason throughout the initial part of the seminar. Twice, the only way the lantern would ignite again was when I prayed publicly, and after a further twiddle, the lamp's mantle flared up to a brilliance too great to look at – an intervention nothing short of the miraculous considering the number of failed attempts before resorting to prayer. The success in igniting the lamp was not lost on the congregation who burst into fervent applause and whoops of delight.

Significantly, that pressure lantern then behaved as all the other lanterns I have used, once the teaching had been really grasped and the Buhid were declaring that they were no longer afraid, for Christ indeed had conquered and would protect those who called on Him in faith. I was convinced Satan had interfered to keep the Buhid at home in their spiritual darkness, away from the light of the liberating word of God.

Although Christians can stand against the demonic by opposing through spoken prayer and scripture (as Christ demonstrates in his wilderness encounter with Satan, an attitude that we should also emulate – 1 Peter 5:8–9), nevertheless I also followed the recommendation, made by those more experienced in dealing with the demonic, that the Buhid should also renounce any past dealing in the occult. The renunciation was not only to cover their own dabbling, but that too of their ancestors who had satanic dealings in their pagan environment. This was prudent because in just a very few cases, we noted that some believers did not always enjoy the freedom their Christian birthright provided when coming into the new life in Christ. Occasionally some dark shadow was still cast over aspects of their lives. Some teachers, considered to be an authority on matters of the occult, cite God's warning, given in the ten commandments, to those who engage in idolatry and the consequent effect it has on succeeding generations:

> "You shall not bow down to them [idols] or worship them; for I, the Lord your God, am a jealous God, punishing the children for the sin of the fathers to the third and fourth generation of those who hate me, but showing love to a thousand generations of those who love me and keep my commandments." (Exodus 20:5–6)

By some, this is taken to mean that when someone is engaged in the occult, not only will he or she be punished, but also the succeeding three to four generations will be at enmity with God, irrespective of whether they too are idolatrous.

That view though suggests a sense of hopelessness, that if a person wants to respond to God within four generations of someone who hated God and had indulged in the dark and secret ways of Satan, then such a person is still labelled as a "God-hater" and cannot be born again. Clearly much evidence is to the contrary.

The offspring of idolaters and God-haters do come into a saving relationship with Christ and have been marvellously set free from the darkness enveloping their parents. They do walk in newness of life and grow in spiritual stature and maturity.

Whilst the Lord's condemnation stands over a pagan people given over to detestable practices, the unmistakable truth is that God's curse ceases when the gospel light shines and men and women choose to come towards Him from out of the darkness.

Jeremiah was informed by God of a future time when the old covenant would give way to a new one:

"In those days people will no longer say:
'The fathers have eaten sour grapes, and the children's teeth are set on edge.' Instead, everyone will die for his own sin; whoever eats sour grapes – his own teeth will be set on edge." (Jeremiah 31:29–30)

Accordingly, under the new covenant, the former punishment extending to three to four generations no longer applies, for every individual will be responsible for his or her own sins and not for those of their forefathers.

However, this does not refute the fact that individuals, having come to faith, are sometimes hindered by events they are not responsible for, nor have any control over. Christa was one such example. Both her grandfather and her father-in-law were practitioners of the occult and their influence reached her, maybe by way of a curse. Another family comes to mind. Although both parents and their many children became Christian, none of them matured in the church. Even when some of their children married keen Christians and went off to live in other villages and attended strong churches, they continued to be stunted as though something were hindering them. Another example was two sisters who had married Christians and had left their pagan environment to live close in a churched community. Although the girls professed to be believers, they were quite unable to pray, even privately. I learned their father was a shaman.

Some of the individuals cited above, whilst being faithful churchgoers, may not have been regenerate and naturally showed no sign of spiritual growth other than adhering to the expectations of the Christian community in terms of church attendance. But in certain cases, the darkness does hold Christians back, for I have seen long-standing believers suddenly grow after they have identified a link with the occult and gone on to renounce it.

The occult dealings which ensnared the Buhid included the placing of curses on people through various means such as the pointing of the finger of death at an adversary, or the gathering of the dust where an enemy's footprint had been left and whispering a death curse over this. There are many such curses. Many could be applied to an area of land, that should anyone gather from it or farm it in successive generations, the farmer would contract an illness that often proved fatal.

All sorts of snares needed to be identified and renounced if the struggling Buhid were truly to make a fresh break. Dark powers were reasserting their insidious influence over the church.

Not all these powers were outwardly destructive. Some were used for the so-called good of the community, such as the healing of the sick through chanting to the spirits of the dead, or the physical removal of demonic darts that had caused otherwise incurable illnesses. The devil selected a few who could see where something was that had either been lost or stolen, or could see the actions of others who were literally miles away and even eavesdrop on their conversation. The list of abominable practices did not end there either but included divination, the reading of omens, observing taboos, interceding as a medium, and the killing of newly born children by burying them alive. Such a list appears in Deuteronomy 18:9–11, which concludes with the reminder:

"Anyone who does these things is detestable to the Lord, and because of these detestable practices the Lord your God will drive out those nations before you. You must be blameless before the Lord." (Deuteronomy 18:12–13)

I felt no fascination while studying the occult. Rather, my study inspired an anger against these things that had so successfully duped generations of Buhid, keeping them in a tight satanic hold of fear and bondage. Worse still, I feared for some who instructed me in these matters, for they would sometimes become fascinated all over again just by re-telling. I would stop them and pray to break the power that seemed veritably to be coming over them again. The satanic force and fascination was something like the ring exerted over the bearer as told in Tolkien's epic, *The Lord of the Rings*. Sometimes I cut my informants short once I had heard enough to understand what the issues were, as too much talk was producing the very thing I was eager to eradicate. Curiosity in this attractive package of secret knowledge always comes with strings attached, guaranteed to further ensnare. In this matter, I was a poor anthropologist for I rarely ventured to get the full picture. I believe the Lord restrained me.

By the final Sunday of the seminar in Manihala, we had reached the last part of the course, a sermon on the armour of God from the closing chapter of Ephesians. I recalled my language blunder when I first preached on the armour of God in Batangan a good two years previously. I had been helping Alexandra to purge the community of intestinal worms and the word for these parasites in Tagalog is "bulate". Now I knew the Tagalog for armour was "baluti", but when I came to the part where I had wanted to say that the believer needs to cover himself daily in the armour of God, I chose the wrong word and said "bulate" instead of "baluti". I had stated the Christian's need to cover himself with the intestinal worms of God! Everyone was straight-faced for a long moment, until I saw one young man beside himself with amusement, literally shaking with silent laughter. An older man sat before me, with a quizzical expression over his face, perhaps thinking that if we were made in the image of God then God also had intestinal worms! Monay saved the day by clearly saying "baluti", the word I had intended to say – "armour" – upon which the entire congregation felt free to laugh. Ever since then, in my nervousness at the start of a sermon, I still sometimes get horribly confused between the two words, although ask me at any other time and there is no confusion in my mind.

On the giant chalkboard of the Manihala church, I had already drawn two life-sized combatants: a Buhid, in just his loin cloth, running to meet his foe – a fangablang, the most powerful and ferocious of all the spirit beings. The fangablang is usually depicted as armed with a long spear, but for the sake of a more biblical connection, I had him, as Satan, firing flaming arrows at the Buhid. The Buhid were fascinated at this picture which extended right across the rear of the church, and you could sense the mounting anticipation as the sermon time approached. They were thinking, quite rightly, who in their right mind would charge at a fangablang bare-handed? And that was one of the points of the sermon, that in our own strength, the Christian is no match to oppose the devil, for we cannot withstand his flaming arrows without heavenly protection.

The second point was that the heavenly armour is already provided but it is the believer's responsibility to put it on. They watched with growing fascination as their representative on the board was transformed from near-nakedness, into a warrior suited in Roman armour. They now began to realise that with the godly armour in place it was not so foolish to go and meet the foe, and of our need to "be strong in the Lord and in his mighty power". This led Paul to exhort: "Put on the full armour of God so that you can take your stand against the devil's schemes." (Ephesians 6:10.)

I related how Buhadan of Siyangi had seen a fangablang waiting for him on a rock outside his house, as he was about to leave for the fields one day. The ferocious spirit sat there tall and erect, clasping a long spear and was accompanied by the usual dog. Buhadan was terrified. But then he remembered the command accompanied by a promise in James 4:7 "Submit yourselves, then, to God. Resist the devil, and he will flee from you". He had at first considered himself a dead man, for no one encountering a fangablang could avoid him, and no mortal could escape with his life. But Buhadan was a man of growing faith and the word of God was clear and could only be certified by putting it to the test. He froze, crouching in the doorway, midway in leaving his house. The fangablang was waiting for him on the stone, fixing Buhadan with his horrible, murderous glare.

"Lord Almighty, I face my fiercest foe, but what is he to you? Come and deliver me. In the mighty name of my Lord Jesus – Amen!"

Buhadan looked up and saw the rock empty where his adversary had been seated just moments before. The fangablang was not there. He couldn't have hidden in the forest, for it was far away. Buhadan rose with a sense of deliverance, but just to make sure, he went around the back of his house. But the fangablang was not there either. His heart welled up with relief and joy and praise.

That evening, in the prayer request time at church, Bagaw raised the question of their whole community moving onto another plot of land much further down the mountain side, which had become available at an affordable price if everyone bought their own piece. The benefits were two fresh water springs that gushed out of the hillside surrounded by clumps of bamboo, providing all the water needs of the community, even towards the end of the dry season. Their present site used to have a natural spring until the Mindoro earthquake of 1994. The earthquake had disturbed rock strata where underground channels had previously flowed with water. With the build up of water pressure, other courses were found, issuing from new outlets gushing out onto the open hillsides. With the proposed village site being much closer to the lowlands, the Manihala community argued in favour of the move, making it easier to send their children to school or to take their sick to the doctor. It was more convenient too to trade their bananas. The downside was that it was further to go to their fields.

But the major stumbling block though was that the plot occupied the site of a former Buhid cemetery! This had put many off the idea of moving there, at least before they had gained new confidence in the might of the Lord to keep them from harm. The cemetery was also the place where in former pagan times, not so very long ago and still very much part of living memory, they had banished the spirits of the dead who had brought sickness on the living. The bad spirit would leave the sick body and retire to the ground in which it had been buried.

It would indeed be a testing time for the community to move onto such a plot, a test of their faith that they might well have to use against any satanic displays of power. In God's providence, this cemetery plot became available, providing an opportunity not only to obtain a supply of fresh drinking water and closer accessibility to the lowlands, but also to confirm their new-found understanding. This provided the test to establish their trust and confidence in the Almighty Lord by making them face up to the powers of darkness.

I recalled a story told by Arlette, our French co-worker with the Iraya Mangyan, the most northerly tribe on Mindoro, and renowned for being the most timid of all the Mangyan. Arlette was encouraging the tribe to make a clean break from the occult and told us the testimony of one of their church leaders, who, having received the biblical teaching about our secure position in Christ against the powers of darkness, had wanted to put it to the test. He went to the cemetery. The first battle he had already won by overcoming his former fear of the place. He remained there a good while and conquered any remaining fear by knowing the strength of being in the Lord. He saw no ghoulish apparitions, and the sounds he heard terrified him no more because he had confronted the powers of evil, clad in the armour of God.

The Buhid liked that testimony and I believe it helped them make the decision to move onto the cemetery site.

CHAPTER ELEVEN

OPPOSITION

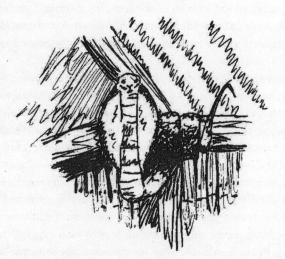

During my visits to Siyangi on my own, I was sleeping in the "guest house", built as a new home by Anaw for his family. Finding that the corrugated iron roof made the house too hot by day and too cold at night, as did several other Buhid who had built themselves new, progressive-style housing, Anaw had opted to remain in his old house. The old house was built of traditional materials from the forest, and the thatch of cogon grass did not accentuate the temperature extremes of day and night. Therefore this new home became the "guest house" and was our home too, since our former house, the one that was the length of my body, had been taken over by another family.

Someone coming into the house in the dead of night awakened me. As Anaw kept a few farming tools in the guest house, I presumed he needed to gather some of these for an early start to reach some land he owned some three hours' walk away from Siyangi. I therefore did not bother to stir from where I was sleeping behind a partition wall, nor even bothered to open my eyes, intent as I was to try to continue with my night's sleep. But within a few seconds of entering the house, he departed again in a hurry, in such haste that he did not bother to close the front door behind him! I got up to close the door and was met by a barrage of questions from my neighbours who were concerned for me, asking whether I was hurt or had been robbed. Anaw himself was among them.

"Two men have just left your house!" they explained. "We were really afraid for you and there was nothing we could do against men with guns. Maybe they were from the NPA camp upriver or maybe they were just brigands. There are a few of them going about Mindoro these days who think nothing of murdering folk first and then helping themselves unhindered to whatever they find!"

What had deterred these men from carrying out an act of robbery, murder or taking me hostage? No Buhid had tried to stop them as they went about their evil business and yet they left abruptly, seconds after entering the house, before reaching my sleeping quarters. I saw and heard nothing to give a clue as to their hasty departure, nor could any of my neighbours say why they fled! Could an angel have opposed them in their tracks and put them to flight in their dismay? I will never know in this life. An angel released Peter from prison. Other would-be robbers and murderers had seen angels when they came to the house of Hazel Page, a former OMF missionary to the Mangyan.

Was not one man – the prophet Elisha – safe even when faced by the might of the Aramean army? "Those who are with us are more than those who are with them" (2 Kings 6:16). God can never be taken by surprise, and evil however rampant can only operate within the permissible will of the Lord who all the time works out His purposes, albeit hidden and mysterious to us at times.

* * *

Whilst reviewing my teaching on Revelation 12 in my hut in Apnagan, reading about the overthrow of Satan, referred to there as a "great dragon" and an "ancient serpent", and of his accompanying rebellious angels being cast out of heaven, I had finally to give in to a call of nature. I had long suppressed the urge, for it was raining, as it had been doing all week, and the climb down to the latrine was treacherous, being steep and slippery. The trip to the latrine also meant using much valuable water afterwards in getting the sticky clay off my feet, water that was difficult to fetch in these conditions. A certain amount of water running off the roof could be collected, but this was not enough for all the foot washing entailed by the coming and going of visiting folk and my daily chores.

The latrine had a woven palm frond roof and sides of flattened bamboo, providing reasonable privacy and shelter, and stood like a booth over the "horrible hole", as one short-term worker named it. I quickly entered the booth and stooped to remove the cover from the hole, and suddenly heard a sound like that of an angry cat spitting in earnest to defend his territory. I rose almost erect, prevented only by the low height of the roof from fully doing so, and looked to confront this angry cat. The sound had come from the bamboo frame at the joint between wall and roof. As I looked through the semi-gloom, I was appalled to see a cobra splay its hood just 18 inches away from my face, threatening me with another horrendous spitting warning, presenting a fearsome view into its mouth.

The cobra was partly wrapped around the horizontal roof support, no doubt having taken shelter inside from all the rain and mud (and who can blame it?) and had probably been resting. After hissing at me, the cobra swung its neck and head back slightly, round to one side. I was mesmerised, petrified into a state of such total inertia that I did not think of making an immediate bid for escape. I felt incapable of taking any action, although in reality this was probably for only about a second, two at the most. The snake lunged suddenly forwards, striking swiftly at my face. That terrifying picture of a snake striking right at my face became an image burned into my mind's eye for weeks after the incident. Every time I closed my eyes to rest, that snake ferociously shot before my eyes, making rest a difficult proposition.

Paralysed as I was by total fear, the snake was sure to get me. Its lightning strike had begun, the cobra was straight on course for my face, and even if I had equally fast reactions, I would not have been able to escape from such a deadly attack.

Next, I found myself lying in the mud six feet out from the latrine, dismayed by what had taken place. The lunging cobra had not bitten me! Before the snake had reached my face, whilst I saw half of its length uncoil as it flew through the gap in the air between my face and the horizontal beam, I found my body suddenly propelled backwards through the open door and out into the mud.

There is no logical explanation for what happened, knowing that a man cannot out-manoeuvre a striking snake under such circumstances. None other than the hand of God snatched me to safety at such a moment, for I never remember having jumped. I watched the cobra slither down a bamboo upright and disappear into the adjacent rice field. Even though I knew the latrine to be safe, I could not bring myself to use it at that moment, nor for a couple of days afterwards.

There are three things I am thankful for. Firstly, the cobra made that spitting sound, alerting me to its presence. Secondly, I was between the door and the snake, facilitating this miraculous, catapult-like escape from the booth. Thirdly, when I came hurtling outside, I still had my trousers on!

White-faced, I went back up the slope and saw my neighbour look at me quizzically, for I was covered in mud. I explained what had happened and since she showed no surprise, seemingly passing it all off with a casual remark about the state my clothes were in all covered in mud, I decided to tell no one else.

After all, what was a snake? The Buhid see them frequently and skilfully dispatch them so what was the big deal? Had I not once been impressed by Gano's total sang-froid at killing a pit viper about to strike his son?

A week later, when I was visiting the Mangyan Bible School up in the north of the island, the principal – who is not a Buhid – happened to remark to me about how God had amazingly protected me from the cobra. I was surprised he had heard, for the news could only have come along the tribal grapevine. My Apnagan neighbour, who I had thought extremely laid back about it all, must have related the incident to another, who in turn told others until the news had travelled the seventy-odd miles to the Bible school in the north.

We do not consider security so much in terms of geographical places of safety, but rather as a spiritual concept of walking with God and being assured of His presence wherever He sends us. His hand is carefully upon us, fulfilling the promise that Christ made at his ascension: "and surely I am with you always, to the very end of the age" (Matthew 28:20), incidentally a promise made to those who obey the call to go and make disciples of all nations (Matthew 28:19).

This helps us to face uncertainty and danger with a confidence that is not from within, but rather comes from a tried and trusted faith in God who has not deserted us in the past nor will forsake us in the future.

Joshua, overwhelmed by the task before him of subduing the people living in Canaan, of facing many battles against well-armed enemies and besieging fortified cities, was given assurance of God's presence and deliverance. He was exhorted to be "strong and courageous" several times. It is a matter of faith, of putting ourselves into God's hands and of crying out to Him at the point of crisis, that has kept us persevering.

There is a sense of our being immortal until God's will is complete! This may sound arrogant, but God has seen us through so many dangers, ranging from TB to a curse of death, from an anti-foreign riot to a striking cobra. God has not concealed us from such dangers. Rather, we have faced them from behind God's shield. We have not gone to the mission field with the misapprehension that nothing bad could ever happen to us. That is totally unbiblical for we only need to look to Christ crucified for us and the ordeals that Paul went through in bringing the gospel to the Roman world (2 Corinthians 6:3–10) to convince us to the contrary.

Obviously there comes a time when the Lord calls us home to be with Him. Stephen was stoned to death whilst preaching the gospel. It is not so much a question of will I be preserved by going to this or that unruly country? It is more an issue of simple obedience: doing what God has clearly indicated, with the accompanying promise of His presence, provides a certain confidence and peace.

The resultant doubt, the uncertainty, even the despair that comes from wilful disobedience to the call of God, is far worse to live with, in my mind, than the uncertainty of facing the dangers of the mission field.

As missionaries, we are very privileged to be so much prayed for. Quite early in our stay one prayer supporter sent us a hand-made card with a verse written in attractive calligraphy on the front, with the words: "Do not be afraid . . . I am your shield, your very great reward" (Genesis 15:1). My wife disagrees that this was the verse, insisting that it said: "Do not be afraid of them, for I am with you and will rescue you" (Jeremiah 1:8), and since we no longer have that card we are unable to convince the other as to which verse was written on the card! Be that as it may, both verses have the same message of the Lord's protective hand over us and so we should not be afraid. The card eventually was delivered to us in Batangan by hand, having been passed from person to person, collected from the post office in Bongabong two or three weeks earlier. The accompanying letter had been opened and part of it was missing, a part we subsequently received on a later visit when others had got bored reading it and decided we could have it.

The point is that we received the card on the day that the NPA moved into town. That night a church elder advised us to move on in the early hours of the morning as they could not guarantee our safety! We were new at that time to the tribes and, still being largely unknown, it was therefore a fairly precarious position to be in, in a society where safety is evaluated by being known for who and what you are.

This was our second "encounter" with the rebels and we were understandably a little apprehensive. As we put our children down to bed on the floor of our hut, Alexandra spotted the card that had the verse saying not to be afraid. Later in the evening as I was tidying up for our early departure, I too came across the card and noted the appropriateness of that verse. As we settled down together for the night, Alexandra prayed, mentioning how mean-ingful the verse was to her and what a comfort it had been arriving at such a time as this, sentiments which were precisely my own.

We both confessed that when we first read the card earlier in the day, before we knew of the arrival of the NPA, the verse had not been particularly significant and one which we could not even recall until we both happened to reread it later. How God had orchestrated things just to give assurance to his anxious children, not only by inspiring a prayer partner to send it with no idea of how significant it would be in bringing courage at a troubled hour, but also by drawing the card to our attention that evening. Even the delay in its delivery ensured its arrival on the day that it was needed! That night we slept soundly and we were out on the trail in the faint light before dawn the following morning, evading an unwanted face-to-face encounter with the rebels.

I cannot deny that there were frustrations, for this whole secur-ity issue did sometimes limit our movements. Perhaps there is a balance here of being wise and listening to others, accepting certain limits not only to avoid compromising one's own security but that of others too. Yet we tried not to allow this to become a screen to hide behind, lest we fear to venture where there might be the slightest risk of danger. We tried to assess the level of the risk together with the Buhid, much as the apostles did before sending Paul away to Tarsus from Jerusalem.

But, contrarily, there seems also to come a time to throw caution to the wind, to ignore the advice of others. Paul rejected the pleas of the disciples at Tyre (Acts 21:4) and went on to Jerusalem where indeed he was bound and taken as a prisoner to Rome. Was Paul right to walk into that viper's nest awaiting him at Jerusalem? Would God have had him heed the advice of the church in Tyre who "through the Spirit" urged him not to go? And how could the Spirit urge them to tell Paul not to go when Paul claims that the Spirit compelled him to go to Jerusalem (Acts 10:22)?

These are questions without answers, I suspect. Paul was a Spirit-driven man, who, shunning his own safety and comfort, became a model for all missionaries. It is well for any missionary facing similar threats, to declare with Paul: "I only know that in every city the Holy Spirit warns me that prison and hardships are facing me. However, I consider my life worth nothing to me, if only I may finish the race and complete the task the Lord Jesus has given me – the task of testifying to the gospel of God's grace" (Acts 20:23–24). One thing is clear, if Paul had been overcautious, the gospel would not have penetrated so many places till much later. It is evident that God was with him in all of this.

We have been fortunate that almost all of the opposition we have encountered has been from lawless people – shamen – and of the natural kind like the cobra, and not from fellow Christians. Possibly some of these foes have been orchestrated by the main adversary keen to silence God's word, who in the long run was unable to succeed.

About half of all the major instances of opposition took place during that memorable year when I went to the villages without Alexandra, the year in which we saw significant breakthroughs. That was our final year when Alexandra was home-schooling Hannah at our Bongabong home. Rarely have we faced opposition from within the church except in one place. A capable church leadership once resented our being there, perhaps because it suggested to them that we considered them incompetent to look after their own affairs. Maybe they were jealous of the attention our visits and teaching received from the church members, who unfortunately set far more store on what the missionary said rather than on instruction from one of their own kind? Most of these leaders pointedly did not attend the teaching during the week, putting in an appearance at weekends only because there would be too many questions asked by others if they failed to come then when the rest of the village was in church. To our faces though, these leaders had the silken speech of flatterers, seeming to be in accord with us.

God very graciously defused this sensitive situation. Each of the men, with the exception of one, eventually responded to my visits to their homes when we talked and prayed over their concerns. Each in turn began to come faithfully to the teaching and worship meetings twice daily. God's word spoke to the hardness in their hearts, exciting them to a renewed zeal for the Lord. The one adamant individual who never really accepted me was ambivalent in his regard to the teaching. Much as he appeared to struggle with me, there were still times when he was supportive of the teaching, recognising the authenticity of God's word. I was glad of these reconciliations.

Ernesto, my OMF colleague, was the one who taught me the value of harmony among God's people. There were times when we did not always see eye to eye. Under stress, the cause of a dispute can be magnified out of all proportion. Always committed to going the extra mile, Ernesto accommodated our concerns and struggles, making the effort to see things from our point of view and being keen to come up with practical solutions. He taught me not to be too idealistic, or to insist that such issues should not arise among Christians, let alone fellow missionaries.

I recall him coming to stay with me overnight in Siyangi, a place he had wanted to visit. Instead of going on a round of visiting folk in their homes, as he was in the habit of doing, naturally gifted as he was in getting along with young and old, he chose to linger with me beside the river. We had just bathed and laundered our clothes and, knowing my heart was burdened for my son Iain struggling with settling down into a new dorm situation in Manila, Ernesto wanted to address the issue.

He went to some length to appreciate the situation, and he too shared his concerns for his youngest son who was going through an unsettled period in Singapore. He shared as an equal and wanted prayer as much for his son as he wanted to pray for Iain. It was that ability to open his heart as a leader, be vulnerable, as well as to feel the other's hurt, that formed a deep bond between us.

* * *

A group of about eight moved swiftly and without word past our house, two of them carrying something wrapped up in a rush mat. Alexandra and Hannah had joined me on this trip to Batangan, where the provision of a table and chair made home-schooling that much more possible. We had arrived in the late afternoon of the previous day and had been in a ceaseless flurry of attending to people's needs, as well as seeing to the many household chores. We had just settled finally to eating lunch after the usual busy Sunday morning of teaching the youth and giving the Bible message, and were looking forward to enjoying some family time. The large double windows were open behind our table to catch the slightest hint of a breeze on that hot, still day and it was through these that the now familiar scene of a funeral procession had been spotted.

I told Alexandra to go ahead with lunch without me, as I went to investigate who had died. Even as I walked over to the church to join the mourners, I sensed it was probably Christa, the girl who had been delivered from demonic interference nearly two years before.

The Buhid do not waste time in burying their dead, not embalming them like the Luktanon do, keeping the corpse in the home for up to ten days for an appropriate time of mourning. The Buhid bury their dead the same day. But even by Buhid standards, this funeral was unusually swift. Christa, we learnt, had been alive when the family attended church just earlier that morning but when they had come back and found her dead, they placed her in an old mat and had it sewn up in the time it had taken us to prepare our simple, cold lunch.

This then was how it all ended. Christa's father was at the front of the church, alone, not wanting to communicate with anyone, and others respected his need to be detached. Christa's mother did not come. Nilo, Christa's husband, turned up at church towards the very end. The only other immediate family member there was Christa's twelve-year-old sister, the only one crying, surrounded by her friends attentively listening to what she shared between sobs.

After the simple funeral service, the corpse was carried out to the forest across the river, involving a climb up a very steep hillside overgrown with jungle. There a hole was dug, after lengthy discussion by all in attendance as to the whereabouts of all the surrounding graves, unmarked except by a sapling. But since this was in the thick of the jungle and there being much natural regeneration of the forest anyway, it was difficult to distinguish what had been planted by previous funeral parties from the steady progression of the forest! I always braced myself for the worst at these grave digs. Thankfully a corpse was never unearthed in my presence.

Christa's grave was prepared, as it worked out, just above where her brother had been laid to rest. He had died at the same age about two years previously. Christa's young adult life had been marred by tragedy, for this brother had broken his spine after the two of them had been larking about in the house and he had fallen out backwards through the door from the raised house. We had first met Christa at this brother's bedside in the hospital in Roxas, nursing the paralysed teenager. He had only survived a week and was brought home to die. Now she was being interred beside the loved brother. The father told me afterwards that a third child of theirs had also died in his late teens.

Had Satan had the final word? This was an unexpected ending

to what had begun with a once-and-for-all deliverance from the clutch of the demons, making us question for a while the degree of freedom Christa had received. Her death was a very sobering reality, especially following the occasion when Monay, sensing the Lord's closeness as we anointed Christa with oil, had hoped for better times. How we wished it had been an example of the power of God not only in deliverance, but also in sustaining those who have crossed over from the demonic to freedom.

As for Christa, her suffering was over and she was now with the Lord. Even though she had been freed from the terrorising demons, Christa had borne the consequences: a damaged back. Her very meek personality had broken through that and other ordeals that few of her tender age have had to endure. To look at the situation in terms of this world only, her pathetic life seemed to little avail, the salvation gained giving little evidence of regeneration beyond the overcoming of the demonic victimisation. In short, there was not much to commend about Christa's decision to trust in Christ.

Every conversion is a deliverance from the evil one, only it is more marked in some cases than in others, as it was with Christa. The decision to trust Christ sets all on a new course which should be plain to see. The believer is like a vessel that, long caught up in some foul-smelling creek, hoists its sail and sets out to sea. The Spirit blows upon the vessel, fills the sail moving it decisively forward through the polluted waters of the creek towards the open sea. But sometimes the boat does not progress and comes to a standstill as though grounded on a mud flat. Caught in that backwater, the boat remains motionless, resigned to its state. The pilot has second thoughts and shows no further wish to make out to sea where the wind is blowing rather too strong for comfort and the water is marked by racing white horses. Such is the outcome of some who at one time moved forward in response to the Spirit of God before coming to an abrupt halt.

Rufeno, who had had the dream of Alexandra and I standing outside his house beside a cross at the fork in the trails, had clearly begun with that promising accompaniment of specific divine intervention and yet too, like Christa, had never moved on. There are many others too, people who can be seen in churches the world over who never progress and seem to be satisfied with a totally unremarkable Christian life. Apathetic, they become a parody of the revolution that Christ intended in overturning the tables of our old established practices.

Christa had been liberated spiritually from the demonic reach, and now through death, had been entirely freed physically, beyond the reach of danger and calamity, enjoying all the security of being in the very palm of the Lord's hand.

> The righteous perish,
> and no one ponders it in his heart;
> Devout men are taken away,
> And no one understands
> That the righteous are taken away
> To be spared from evil.
> Those who walk uprightly
> enter into peace;
> they find rest as they lie in death.
>
> (Isaiah 57:1–2)

CHAPTER TWELVE

TIME OF WONDER

For a long time, until recently, Sagyom had been leading the small church at Safang Uyang every Sunday, about an hour's walk away along the ridge from Apnagan where he lived. Deciding the believers were mature enough, Sagyom desisted from making these visits in the hope their gifts would emerge more to the fore by being no longer dependent on his help.

I decided it was time I finally paid a visit to this small fellowship of eight believing households, more so upon hearing reports that they were extremely frightened by the powers of darkness.

Many of them there had never owned a Bible before and had sent word to me to bring a number of Bibles along to sell. They had problems finding the relevant text to our studies. By this time I had learned not to skip about the scriptures, and made a point of teaching in expository fashion whenever possible, with most of the cross-references written up on the board. Although I had given them an overview of how to find certain Bible books more easily, explaining the division of Old and New Testaments and drawing their attention to the table of contents at the beginning, they still struggled initially. I went around assisting them, turning to the right page, instructing them individually, and placing a sheet of paper between the two Testaments to avoid them laboriously ploughing through the Old Testament in search of a New Testament book. In spite of this there would still be a frantic rustling of pages being turned over after I had deemed it an appropriate time to start. Their eagerness and anticipation kept me from even the slightest irritation.

On the Sunday, when I had been preaching a good ten minutes, a timid woman came apologetically up the divide between the two rows of pews and placed her open Bible down on the pulpit: "Faduwasay – show me where you are speaking from. It's important what you are saying and I must know where I can read this to remind myself later!" What joy it was to have such a responsive congregation, anxious to understand, intent to follow in their Bibles, keen to underline meaningful verses. The teaching addressed their fear of the demonic by looking at Christ's supremacy over the powers of darkness.

My coming to Safang Uyang was considered a special occasion, for their village was small and they presumed their little church too insignificant. They made the most of my visit, wanting me to lengthen the teaching sessions, and individuals summoned the boldness to seek me outside of these times. Even the teenagers, inspired by God's word, found the courage to ask me to teach them to read and, once they got started, they implored me to make time for another reading session later in the day. These teenagers were not totally illiterate, but certainly lacked the confidence and know-how to attempt to read on their own. They lacked the backing and practical help too from the literate. By the end of the nine days, two out of three of the teenagers were ecstatic about being able to manage on their own and went on to be baptised soon afterwards.

Sayna, the main elder at Safang Uyang, and Eba his wife, were my very good hosts. They had provided a low-roofed store room as my own home, separate from their own place. Every meal time, Sayna or one of their children brought me over a plate of rice and vegetable stew. One lunchtime he asked me: "Would you be prepared to come with me to the two households of those who are still chanting to the spirits of the dead? They are close by."

I agreed.

"Then perhaps we could go at about quarter to five this afternoon. That will probably be the time when they are back from their fields!" Sayna surprised me with his frequent reference to precise time, for none of the other Buhid took any notice of timekeeping. He had a heavy-looking, gold-coloured watch, his pride and joy.

Besides the many natural reasons for the villagers' interest, the Spirit of the Lord was very noticeably present. Their attention in the meetings can only be described as avid, fired by spiritual longing to be set free from fear, to know the reality of the risen Christ and find a bold faith. A sense of desperation to understand God's word made Bible study their first priority, and all other activities of the day were centred around their request for the maximum number of hours I was able to teach. They regarded this visit as their one-off opportunity to get to grips with spiritual reality.

The fellowship was unlike anything I have ever experienced anywhere else, for all were of one accord, one in mind and spirit. I felt enveloped in a warm cloud of brotherliness, a fine harmony that I was acutely aware of. The entire congregation immediately walked into this sacred atmosphere upon entering that tumble-down shack of a church and became wrapped up in it themselves. It veritably seemed that the shekinah presence of the Lord was there, transporting each one of us out of our squalid, muddy environment and setting us up upon the glassy sea before the throne of God.

Our singing was not great, for we were not many in number and they had not inherited the musical skills of the Apnagan church.

Nor was my teaching brilliantly presented. But the teaching was anointed. An anointing that not only enabled me to speak with much freedom and clarity, but an anointing that opened the ear, heart and soul of every Buhid who came into that building.

Anointing, as I have learned from such experiences, is as much to do with the hearer's ability to listen with the inner ear as it is to do with the preacher's ability to speak beyond his own limitations and resources. In short, it was not of me, nor was it contrived by the congregation, but was of God, a product of His tangible presence that held us rapt and in awe.

Anointing has much to do with personal consecration and cannot be expected where there is prayerlessness, nor unconfessed sin on the part of the preacher. Anointing is more likely to occur where there is prayerful, passionate striving for the majesty and glory of the Lord to be revealed, where there is hunger for more of God, irrespective of the cost, and a realisation that for all our studying and expertise, we are quite incapable ourselves of reproducing any semblance of real anointing.

I do not mean to be arrogant, nor wish to boast as though I had a large part in all of this. It is a sad reflection and indictment upon my ministry with the Buhid that such anointing was not a more common feature. It is notable that the period of anointing was during this final year that we spent with the Buhid (with the exception of a very few isolated instances such as in the beginning at Siyangi), and, sadly for Alexandra, took place whilst she was more or less confined to Bongabong in home-schooling Hannah.

I have to be very careful in the way that I write the following. I would suggest that this blessing had a connection with being on my own! I spent most of my free time in prayer when I was not too exhausted and had to sleep. When Alexandra and I were together in the hills, we naturally spent time talking to one another, time which, when I was on my own, I spent praying. Alexandra's presence meant having extra visitors, women who had come to speak and pray with her. Alexandra is a gifted conversationalist, and visitors stayed longer when she was around.

Also, being on my own, I tended to simplify meals, sometimes making do with a drink or eating up a few leftovers rather than going to all the trouble of preparing something fresh. On this practical point there is much to commend fasting.

Although Alexandra and I had times of joint and individual prayer, it was not of the concentrated kind, characteristic of when you are on your own. Much of our modern way of life runs quite counter to the prayerful attitude required if one is to hope for continued times of special anointing. Life is so full of distractions, and because so many of us cannot resist playing and working on our computers, or (I include myself) are given to watching television or any other type of pastime or recreational activity, a good portion of our free time is taken up. Even the pursuit of spiritual things like the perfecting of a sermon, can subtract from time to beseech God and cry out for His blessing. After all, if we think the polished presentation is what is most required, we are saying that it depends more on us and not on God.

This is not to support sloppiness. We rightly should be committed to doing a skilled job, but never at the expense of much soul-searching and prayer for revival. Clearly a balance has to be reached. I am not overstating the point either, for I have heard missionaries solicit prayer in public meetings saying the demands are so great, the pressure of time so demanding that they don't have the opportunity for much prayer themselves!

The blessing was not limited to the church members in Safang Uyang but had a ripple effect in the small community. Mention has already been made of the two teenagers who came to faith and were baptised soon after. The husband of one of the believers also came to the meetings, having been uninterested in church for years, and came to such a saving faith that he told his wife that they should both be baptised as soon as possible. A few weeks later he was falsely accused of murder. When he went to report to the police about a body he had found in a field, the police bullied him to sign a confession, forcing his thumbprints onto a paper to sign the declaration. Through this entire ordeal and the indignity of being in jail, he did not abandon his new faith, but became a man of prayer and trust. Soon acquitted by the intervention of our legal worker and co-missionary, he immediately went on to be baptised, together with his wife.

Sayna came over to me at the end of the afternoon teaching session as arranged. "Faduwasay – it's twenty-five to five. In five minutes, we should make those visits which I spoke of earlier!" I noted that Sayna did not really engage in conversation with the rest of us in the church, but sat detached, periodically studying the face of his watch. All of a sudden, he stood up announcing: "It's twenty to five – time to go!" The other Buhid looked at Sayna vaguely amused, then at me quizzically, assessing whether I was likewise motivated by this passion for punctuality. Noticing my eyes narrowing into a smile, they beamed back at me, without words, sharing their amusement.

To each household we paid a visit. Buhid are most keen that all should be of one accord with regard to spiritual matters. Since the unconverted are still chanting to the spirits of the dead, to demons, a foothold for Satan is perceived, one through which he meddles in the community and tempts weaker Christians to consult those who have shaman powers.

One household began attending church after my departure. Another family, a believing couple having marital problems, openly asked for prayer and were wonderfully reconciled, both exhibiting a grace that was not their own. They too went on to be baptised, together with four others.

Sayna himself was full of the Spirit and had so much enthusiasm that he began to attend inter-church meetings which previously he never had time for. No one was trained to lead the baptismal classes in the church at Safang Uyang, and Sayna felt it would be a long while before someone from Apnagan would come to lead the week-long classes. The Hanselmans, however, in their very thorough way, had beautifully produced the whole series of baptismal lessons covering the essentials of the faith and had this incorporated into the back of the Buhid hymn book together with many other helpful guides, from conducting a marriage to burying the dead, a kind of book of "Common Order". I led Sayna through the content of these lessons until he felt confident enough to use and explain these lessons himself to the baptismal candidates. Classes began as soon as I had left and the six were baptised at a conference in Apnagan just a few weeks later.

Discipling leaders like Sayna was vital for the future health of the church and they were much prayed for. God was abundantly answering prayers for the Buhid saints. God gave them knowledge, through His word, adding wisdom and understanding just as it was with Bado and his prophetic dream of preaching at the front of the church from a Bible turned to stone, open there at the promise of Godly wisdom given to those who ask.

Our ministry was primarily to prepare "God's people for works of service, so that the body of Christ may be built up" (Ephesians 4:12). Such a ministry is often entitled "leadership training". I prefer the term "discipling", because this does not only target obvious potential leaders, but embraces those whom God calls. We discovered we were called to aid the unpromising, the illiterate, the dull, the worldly politician, those defeated by habitual sin. Many were not leadership material in the eyes of man, but through a gracious God, He powerfully raised up leaders from among the "foolish things . . . the weak things . . . the lowly things . . . and the despised things . . . the things that are not – to nullify the things that are, so that no one may boast before him" (1 Corinthians 1:27–29).

Some were leaders already, men like Monay and Sagyom, nurtured by our predecessors, trained and equipped at the Mangyan Bible School. They helped us to understand the needs of the tribal church and provided us with much appreciated fellowship. These mature leaders nevertheless still looked for advice, sought for prayer, and struggled with biblical and wider church issues.

Sayna's father made an unusual request to me.

"Is it alright to pray over a piece of land?" he asked hesitantly. "You see, I acquired this piece of land a long time ago, where a dead person had been abandoned in a house and left to rot. We have feared his spirit, and the land has not been developed because it is believed to be specially cursed!"

I was somewhat hesitant about the appropriate course of action, given the church's controversial debate over territorial spirits. But I could not ignore his request for help, since the curse was a hindrance not only to his land being worked, but to his faith as well. To avoid going onto that land would have meant defeat, and the purpose of expounding the biblical revelation of the supremacy of Christ over the nine days of my visit would have been quite meaningless. I agreed to his request, though I regarded the whole debate as to whether certain spirits were contained to an area or not, as being frankly purely academic. It is naïve to presume Satan has any such geographical limitations. The real issue at stake here was of securing a believer's freedom from the realm of satanic influence.

We went as a group to Sayna's father's land. A good way along the trail to Apnagan (contrary to their saying it was close by), the father led us to the site where a hut had once stood and been abandoned with the corpse. The women and the children hung back, preferring to remain at the trail, for reasons I did not immediately appreciate. We sang some hymns, summarised the content of the believer's secure position in Christ, read some passages of scripture and prayed, formally breaking any curse.

Whilst reading from the Bible, I suddenly felt a sharp and very fiery pain in my foot, making me wince and pause in mid-sentence. The Buhid looked at me with a sense of horror as it dawned on them that the spirit of the dead had probably bitten my foot! Aware of what they were thinking, I picked off the fiery red ant from my foot and showed it to them. They laughed with relief. I wonder whether it was just coincidence? Sayna's father asked if it was safe now for him to work this land and whether women and children could come upon it? In answer to my question, he explained that women and children were more vulnerable to this particular curse, hence only the adult males had ventured onto the site. I was able to reply, with total assurance, that every trusting believer was quite secure. He looked delighted and did not doubt, for, soon after, he worked that land without any ill consequence.

A believer in Siyangi told me of a piece of land he had inherited with a curse upon it. He asked me what he should do about it. I reminded him of our security in Christ and only then did he make the link with the course I had taught some months earlier and the issue of this curse. He rummaged about in a basket hanging from the wall of his home and drew out my printed notes on the subject, waving them about jubilantly on realising their relevance. On his own initiative, he decided to go along with his believing brothers and pray at the land to break the curse.

At the end of the course Sayna approached me. "Faduwasay, you know this is quite an occasion, us all being together," he began, stashing his betel nut in the corner of his cheek to speak more clearly. "Day in and day out, we have been studying the scriptures and singing God's praise and we have found release from our fears. You know – we should have a banquet, just like we do when we Buhid all gather at a conference!" Those sitting with us warmly embraced this idea.

That Friday the church put on a veritable banquet, every household bringing along a pot of rice and a pot of something tasty to go on top. It was a beautiful atmosphere, one of euphoria, and everyone had beaming smiles, even though the rain had not ceased right through my visit and the mud was dreadful. After piling a hill of rice on my plate, everyone came with their pots-of-something-tasty and ladled generous amounts till the plate was literally overflowing. No sooner had I eaten a portion than another ladle would approach my plate, ignoring my polite protests. I had to stubbornly refuse and physically remove my plate from the ladles before they believed I was no longer hungry but quite bursting at the seams. I have never enjoyed a gathering before or since so much as that simple occasion in the mud of Safang Uyang, with a people I had only come to know over the previous eight days, whose background, culture and upbringing were so vastly different from my own. A deep spiritual bond had developed. I felt such an overwhelming love for my brothers and sisters that for once I did not have longings to be back with Alexandra and Hannah.

We completed the banquet by celebrating the Lord's Supper for the first time ever in that church, an event full of significance for those who had just come to faith that week, and marking too a peak in the pilgrimage of the six baptismal candidates as well as those who were already baptised believers.

The next day, after Eba had cooked the usual breakfast of rice and a vegetable stew, Sayna and I made our way back down to the trading post. At last the rain had stopped, the sun was up and a wind blew. Amazingly the clay in places was drying to a more manageable consistency, like that of playdough, making walking easier in the open sections of the trail.

We had reached a bald ridge, clear of any tree or shrub, and the path ran right along the top, shortly before it started its descent to Apnagan. Sayna, who was leading, turned back with a look of horror across his face. He wanted to speak but was unable to in his extreme agitation. He suddenly threw himself to the ground into a foetal position, and desperately motioned me to do the same.

My first thought had been that maybe a snake was about to strike. This thought was quite absurd since snakes do not exert the same sense of terror in the Buhid that they do in me. Besides, throwing ourselves onto the ground before a snake was the last thing to do! But my mind was still scarred from that encounter with the cobra in the latrine.

"What's the matter?" I asked as I flung myself virtually on top of Sayna.

Sayna was still speechless with horror and succeeded only in stretching out an arm to the south. I followed the direction he was pointing and noticed a dark cloud moving towards us. At first I didn't know what to make of it, but it was no ordinary cloud, having a life of its own and changing shape and direction. Maybe it was a cloud of locusts?

"Bees!" exclaimed Sayna, shaking with fear. Then I heard the vibrant drone of tens of thousands of bees making precisely towards the part of the ridge where we were conspicuously lying on the highest eminence. The bees formed a vast swarm, maybe several swarms combined, for they filled the space that a public building would occupy. They were almost upon us. Sayna stopped looking, burying his face into the elbow of his arm. I did likewise and tensely waited. The drone of the bees' wings grew to a fearful pitch as they came upon our ridge, their passing taking an age. Then they were past and Sayna asked if I was all right. We both emerged totally unscathed.

"If I had raised my arm," Sayna said raising his arm above his head, "the bees would have flown into it. They were that close!"

Had this been another attempt of Satan to silence me and to remove the leader of the Safang Uyang church who had just found a dynamic faith? Or was it just another coincidence? Whatever, we were thankful to the Lord and praised Him for delivering us from a potentially fatal situation, giving us more days yet to speak of His glory and power.

CHAPTER THIRTEEN

MOVING ON IN THE LORD

Gano's new house was coming on well. It had been two weeks since he had sunk the thick supporting uprights, that form the stilts, into the ground. Onto these vertical poles were fixed all the horizontal beams for the floor and roof joists, bound by strong vine. Now he was putting on the last of the thatch, bundles of cogon grass secured under a bamboo strip, doubled back, then folded over the top of the bamboo so that it lay flat, pointing down the roof slope.

Gano was not alone. All over the newly acquired cemetery plot that encompassed an open section of steep hillside, the houses of the new Manihala were being erected, all at different stages of progress. Hammer blows periodically sounded, dulled by distance and all the empty space, as bamboo slats were nailed onto the floor joists. The animated banter of small groups of two to three men would rise and fall, as together they set off and came back from the forest with bamboo and straight tree limbs, vine and cogon grass. Wives were involved in some of the building work too when they were not cooking and gathering food and water. For the younger children it seemed like one long permanent holiday, and they had to be coaxed, and quite often spoken to severely, to go and get water. The older children accompanied their fathers in finding materials from the forest, and enjoyed honing their skills, equipping them for fast-approaching adulthood. For the Buhid adulthood begins as early as twelve or thirteen years old, an age when an individual could adequately fend for himself or herself, in all agricultural and domestic activities, including the caring for a family. In communities that have access to a school, marriage tends to be put off until sixteen, eighteen or sometimes beyond.

A sudden shriek rent the air, making everyone look up, wondering whether someone had injured themselves with a fotol or hammer. A young man emerged, running from his house, quite beside himself, and continued to run straight uphill to the next house. He did not appear to be clutching any damaged limb. Gano descended from his roof to see what the matter was.

"I was fixing the floor slats down, nailing them, when all of a sudden a hand thrust itself up through the floor in front of me!" The young man was still breathless, more from fear than exertion.

"Did you see whose hand it was?" asked another.

"It was a dismembered hand, all covered in blood – it was going to throttle me! It was then that I shrieked and ran for my life!" His eyes were wide with fear. His audience teased out all the information that they could, but nothing more was particularly relevant.

"Did you not send up a quick prayer?" suggested Gano.

"No – I was petrified. I ran for my life!"

"Don't you remember the teaching that the demons cannot oppose us once we speak to the Almighty One? The demons cannot stand against the one who places his trust in the Lord."

"I was so scared that I didn't linger to think!" the young man replied with a short nervous laugh.

"Well, the demons don't sort of announce their arrival, do they? They don't clear their throats before coming into the house!" another added to deliberately lighten the atmosphere. One or two laughed, but only briefly, as fear settled over them once more.

"Don't you remember what Faduwasay Martin had said just before he left us after his last visit?" Gano looked around them briefly, allowing time to recall. "He said that we would probably be tested when we moved onto this cemetery ground, especially since we had been studying our Father's words and promises that He is greater by far than all the demons combined and that we are secure in Christ if only we would believe and keep faith!"

"Yes that's right," said another newcomer, "we all took great confidence from what we studied that week. God really spoke to us then!"

"And now God has allowed us to be tested indeed," observed another.

"What should we do?" asked the young man who had seen the dismembered hand.

"Well, what do you think?"

"Pray?"

"Yes," said Gano. "You know, if you had prayed when you saw that hand appear, it would probably have just vanished. Remember that story about Buhadan seeing the fangablang? There and then he prayed and when he had just finished praying and looked up, the fangablang – the mightiest of all the demons – had just vanished!" As Gano reminded them, he looked around at all the faces about him. During this discourse, many more had arrived, summoned by the shriek. Rumour had spread quickly and tools were dropped as well nigh everyone on the site gathered round to listen and comment. By now the account of what had happened had been repeated, and the general opinion was that the young man should have prayed.

Before they went back to their work, Gano led them in prayer, at the end of which they all prayed together, aloud, as was their custom.

In the days that followed a few more ghoulish happenings occurred, some possibly the result of natural phenomena, a frightening sound, a movement in the corner of the eye. The mood in the work camp was tense and expectant, but rather than these supernatural occurrences intimidating the villagers and persuading them to abandon the site, they gained assurance from the scriptures they had underlined that were pertinent to the power of God. Their confidence grew, infecting one another. After a few days, no more ghoulish apparitions were reported and the occasional word about the demonic could well have been attributed to natural causes. The fear had gone and a new-found confidence discovered, as they delighted in the strong, protecting arm of the Lord.

Such was the mood that I found on my next visit to Manihala, this occasion staying for the first time at the new village site in Gano's house. More Bibles were being requested by those who had been on the fringes of the church up until that time. The new site had gathered many formerly isolated households into close proximity with one another, giving the opportunity for the Christians to influence greatly the mood of those who had not made a commitment through their fearless stand against demonic activity. The strong stood with the weak, the faithful prayed with the faithless.

Satan had really shot himself in the foot. His tactics, proven to work with pagans, would have resulted in a death or two, had pagans or weak Christians had the audacity to remain in the cemetery. But he had not considered that these Buhid – greatly apprehensive by nature, although Christian, still wrestling with fear – would have stood firm in the liberating knowledge of the supremacy of Christ, and moreover oppose him through prayer, causing him to retreat. The picture that had been drawn on the chalkboard often came to their mind, of a Buhid dressed only in a loincloth coming to face the might and ferocity of a frightful fangablang armed with a bow and flaming arrows. Formally they acknowledged that in no way could they oppose such demonic power on their own. The drawing on the armour of God, the application of Ephesians six, might have convinced some to stand their ground, but it had not entirely carried weight with the majority. It required their church to be tested, and through the conviction of the mature, the entire church was brought through the valley of the shadow of death, fearing no evil. More were added to the church as a result.

The mood in the new Manihala was buoyant with hope and confidence, liberated from all those centuries-long fears that had set them in bondage to the diabolical deeds of the adversary.

We had no church building as yet, but we met in Gano's substantial house; for having a wide doorway between the two inner rooms, it allowed both rooms to be filled and yet still gave us the sense of being part of one group. Many a testimony was shared, and people I was not familiar with, who normally did not attend the meetings, were now present! Folk who had not yet completed their homes at the new site and were living still at the old one, a good mile and a half away, also attended some of the meetings. The inconvenience of traipsing across from the old village, together with the pressure to complete their new homes, was testimony to the importance they placed on worshipping God.

The singing was beautiful. The girls, who usually sang more ably than the men there in Manihala, sang with a note of confidence, an appreciation that welled up into the surging lilt of the Pacific, a most delicious offering of praise to the Lord. The men were not outdone, for they were now coming into their own, and their less skilled accompaniment sounded equally as fine, for their praise was largely a novel experience, an expression of their new-found freedom. We sang for much longer than usual, enjoying celebrating our Lord together, and no one complained or thought it too long; nor did it impinge on the time spent on Bible study.

At the time of my previous visit, they had asked me to teach a seminar about Christian marriage. They still wanted teaching on this but their thoughts were also upon the "end times" as we had just entered the new millennium. Due to their keenness to study, combined with the incessant rain as the Philippines experienced its second consecutive year of the La Niña phenomena (rain throughout the dry season), we ran a third session each day. This allowed time to study some scriptures pertaining to the cosmic struggle between the forces of evil and Christ; the satanic world system pitted against the seemingly insignificant Church. This was not the systematic expository style teaching done in Apnagan, but more a dipping into appropriate texts suitable for a less mature and less knowledgeable congregation.

Such "end times" studies can be very academic, detached from the here and now, exciting all kinds of idle curiosity and conjecture, and of little practical help to our daily walk with the Lord. Not so in Manihala. They grasped the key issues of the need to remain faithful under the mounting pressures of the secular world, tensions ranging from the sometimes unjust state judicial system, biased against Christians, to episodes of violent persecution to repress and stamp out the Church. God's righteous wrath, which appalls so many Western readers of Revelation, comforted the Buhid – as I would imagine it reassures so many Christians the world over, who are discriminated against, who are the marginalised, considered the scum of society, without a voice to be heard. Such people tame their own wrath by adhering to God's command: "Do not take revenge, my friends, but leave room for God's wrath." They can leave their own indignation with the Lord, knowing that He will bring people to account.

These young believers, elated still by the deliverance that the Lord had brought their whole community through, impressed upon me the need to keep faithful whatever the cost. Gano passionately declared to us all:

"If the NPA or anyone else for that matter, come for me with their guns and all their authority to persecute me for being a Christian, I will not turn and run. I will not deny my Lord for I know Him and cannot be separated from Him. I will gladly lay my life down and by doing so, my persecutors may be convinced too of there being a Lord to whom they too must one day give account." His wife giggled nervously before nodding her head in assent. How she must have marvelled at the pace his faith was growing, indeed overtaking her own.

"I w-w-would do the same," declared Hogday struggling with a stammer that afflicted him particularly when he became animated about a matter. "My only hope is that they would k-k-kill me quickly, just a bullet in the head and that would be it. I would fear being tortured. Although they might t-t-torture me, I would not deny Christ. He is my everything, my all in life, He it is who has given meaning to my life."

"I would like to think I would not be afraid," declared Mercy, biting her lower lip thoughtfully, "but I am afraid that I might be afraid!"

Her statement was met with a brief salvo of laughter before everyone returned to their deep meditation.

Who knows how he or she will behave on the day of persecution? But I sensed these oaths and vows were real at that precise moment, that had the NPA burst into our hut and said, "All those who do not follow Jesus get out now for we are going to burn down this house", I do believe that most of them would have remained sitting just where they were, to be consumed in the flames singing praise to God. I was persuaded that this was not the language of bravado, but an acknowledgement of how much Christ had come to mean to so many of them.

"Because of the increase in wickedness, the love of most will grow cold, but he who stands firm to the end will be saved," read Gano from Matthew 24:12–13. "There it is," he announced with conviction, "that is the very heart of the teaching about the end times. We should memorise it!"

All were struck by the same conviction, those two verses summarising in a nutshell, the intent of the passage and they immediately set to memorising the section. Soon everyone was saying it with a note of defiant triumph as they recited the verse without hesitation.

"Faduwasay!" Kaw-kaw, Hogday's wife, attracted my attention. She knitted her brows. "What does this mean: 'How dreadful it will be in those days for pregnant women and nursing mothers!' Is it wrong to be married?"

They were now voicing their concerns, airing their struggles in understanding the text, and if they still felt embarrassed about their ignorance it no longer mattered as much as the importance of understanding God's word. I was able to assure Kaw-kaw, and others too timid to ask, that Jesus was referring only to the difficulty and suffering that would be experienced and was in no way judging those who had married and had children. God had clearly intended Adam to have Eve as a wife, and for mankind to multiply. Kaw-kaw looked relieved.

"Tell us more about the meaning of the 666." The fact that they said "666" in English, with an uncertain accent, alerted me to the fact that they had probably picked this up from conversations with Luktanon who enjoyed throwing in a bit of English now and then to show off in front of those they considered their inferiors. The Buhid did not as a rule understand English, although a few bright ones, the ones attending high school in the last few years, did have a knowledge of English, but never used it with us. These folk in Gano's house did not speak English.

I had learned early on never to presume scriptural knowledge. We turned to Revelation 13 and I emphasised our need always to start from scripture, not from what someone else had said about the Bible. We read about the beast forcing everyone to receive the 666 mark upon them if they were to buy or sell.

This piece of information was received with a high note of exclamation which dropped in intonation. This was then followed by much clicking of their tongues to express surprise and dismay. They asked questions to clarify.

"Although it would be difficult for us Buhid in those days, it won't be as hard for us as it will be for others. The only things we really do need, that we cannot get from the land, are salt and matches!"

I reminded them that they didn't need matches, for the Bangon in particular make do with a flint struck upon metal, igniting dry inflammable material like kapok or wood shavings.

Hogday, the one with the stammer, used this pause in the proceedings to relieve himself outside. Gano turned to me to ask:

"What would happen if we were to elect one of us, say Hogday, to receive the 666 sign? Could we then give him our orders for what we wanted from the market? Could he sell our bananas for us?"

I was not sure whether Gano was being serious. I was inclined to laugh, but noticing their serious expressions, I realised the question was in earnest.

"Just think of the implications of your suggestion. Look at what it says in the fourteenth chapter of Revelation, verse nine." I paused whilst everyone looked up the reference. " 'If anyone worships the beast and his image and receives his mark on the forehead or on the hand, he, too, will drink of the wine of God's fury, which has been poured full strength into the cup of his wrath.' It would mean that Hogday would not be saved and would be eternally separated from the rest of us."

At that moment, Hogday came back into the house. "What's this you're saying? What is this about me?" he managed to stammer out, scanning our faces with much curiosity. One or two began to laugh which only increased his consternation. Since no one seemed to want to volunteer the information, I thought it best to put him out of his suspense.

"They were considering whether you could receive the 666 mark so that you could lead about twenty water buffalo down the trail to the market, sell all of Manihala's bananas to the dealers, and with the money buy everything written down on a shopping list and carry all that rice and fish and laundry soap and paraffin back up the hill again and distribute it to the twenty or so households here!"

"W-w-w-when will I have to d-d-do this?" The poor man looked confused, but bless his heart, he seemed earnestly to consider the possibility of fulfilling this outrageous suggestion. We soon set his mind at rest and he joined his hearty laughter with the rest of us. However, Hogday, sitting next to Gano, made a point of pinching the nerves at the base of his friend's rib cage for coming out with the outrage in the first place. Gano squirmed and writhed under Hogday's pretend torture until the latter desisted.

It was the timid Mercy, quietly spoken, her soft face radiant with an inner beauty of a soul at rest with the Lord, who brought our discourse to an end. She drew our attention back to a passage we had looked at the previous day:

"You know we will be afraid if we have to face such times, but we should fear God's judgement more than the wrath of man. I have just been re-reading this from 1 Peter: 'Since you call on a Father who judges each man's work impartially, live your lives as strangers here in reverent fear.' Our life is only short. We can't hold onto it at all costs, nor should we, for what is it compared with eternity with God in heaven?"

"Yes even if there be hours of torture," declared Gano, "that will be soon forgotten when enjoying the eternity in our Father's house, of no more pain and injustices."

I take issue with those who say that the biographies of the giants in the faith like Hudson Taylor and Amy Carmichael are glossy, unrealistic portraits of unbelievably spiritual Christians. It is sometimes inferred that it is no longer practical or possible for us to be like-hearted! Some biographies are unreal, showing only the positives. But the spirituality of men and women of this stature, of the kind characteristic of some at Manihala, complete with their own frailty and faults, is real. They have been consumed by a passion for Christ in a way that does not characterise many contemporary Christians. They have seen the glory of the Lamb and will settle for nothing less, no counterfeit experience. They are like the trader in the parable who, having seen the pearl of great value, have sold all their possessions to acquire it. Not drawn by the fads of fashion, they are devoted to reading the Bible and not all the many spiritual books of the "How to . . ." variety. It is still possible to be committed in this respect, but it is without doubt costly, liable to make us misunderstood, often forcing us to go against the tide and be regarded as something of a crank outside of mission circles.

* * *

On one of the drier days, I accompanied Gano to the former village of Manihala to see some of the older believers, who would be around during the day and had not yet moved to the new site. Gano had to attend to some fields further on and left me there in the village. I had also wanted to collect some of my belongings from the house that Gano had built for us, but more than that, I greatly desired to rest there a few hours, enjoy the magnificent view of the coast and reef below, the islands diminishing in size to specks out in the vast tropical seascape under the unusual lucidity of the sky that day. First I made my visits and sorted through the business of medicine sales, drawing up an inventory with the health carer. Then I entered the sanctuary of that home.

The week had gone well, with so many encouragements to praise God for, the all-important breakthrough in the community as they took a united stand in the victory of Christ over the powers of darkness, and now their thirst for more of God, transcending the wants and desires of this life. How far they had come from almost three years before, when they were on the verge of ship-wrecking their uncertain faith by joining the Iglesia ni Cristo sect with its blasphemous denial of the Lordship of Christ. There would be no turning now in this camp. Now they could show one another the scriptures, for guidance and correction. I spent a good while praising God until fatigue got the better of me.

Gano's return to our old house stirred me from my mingled state between slumber and basking in all of the goodness of what God had accomplished before me. He nimbly entered with his beaming smile and sat next to me to enjoy the view he so admired and had given me as a gift by blocking it out – in the building of this hut for my family – from the window of his own home.

"I am sad that I will no longer stay in this place!" I remarked looking out of the window onto the glorious panorama.

After a few moment's hesitation, Gano replied: "I am going to build a new house next to mine, for you and your family to stay in." I looked at his earnest expression. "It's sad they're not able to be with you during your visits. We are happy when you and your whole family come here."

"No, you had better not build a new house for us just now. You know we will be going back to our country in less than six months' time and when we return again, God willing, a year later, it is a little unknown exactly what our ministry will be. There is a lot of talk about my teaching in some of the other tribal churches. Some of these have been without missionary help for years and are in a state of decline."

I assured Gano, as I did many others, looking ahead to the next term of missionary service, that the Buhid would not be abandoned, that they had a very special place in our hearts, and that, God willing, in so far as it depended upon us, we would still come to be with them, only less frequently. We planned what the church would like me to teach on my next and last visit, this side of our year's return to Scotland. (That visit never took place, for I came down with dengue fever just before my proposed plan to climb up to Manihala.)

Gano was silent for a while, evidently deep in thought, aware that the era of my frequent visits was coming to an end. Gano still liked to read the Bible to me, to practise his reading skills. Now understanding what he read, he was full of questions. He responded well to completing reading assignments. In the three months between visits, Gano would have read two to three Old Testament books and would passionately discuss these with me. "Why were the Israelites so blind and stupid not to follow God after they had seen His power and glory?" Gano would ask me incredulously.

"You know," began Gano, "I have been thinking for a while

about Deborah and me going to the Mangyan Bible School. Deborah's sister, Hokabid and Fodo, her husband, also have the same thought. You know what I would most like to do? I would like to go and move home right up the Aliyanon River and over the hills into the west of the island. I have some unbelieving relatives living there and I would like to share the gospel with them."

I encouraged Gano in his noble aims and we prayed together, asking the Lord to keep us steadfast in His purposes.

Many like Gano showed an Isaiah-like obedience. They had now seen the Lord in His glory and had heard the heavenly anthem swell in their ears with the cries of "Holy, holy, holy!" Aware of their own sinfulness they had stood before the Lord, naked and ashamed, for nothing was concealed before His intense, all-seeing gaze. The compassionate Lord had removed their disgrace, just as the hot coal had touched Isaiah's lips, cleansed his unwholesome tongue. So they too felt clean and renewed. Their eyes were filled with His wonder and their hearts were singing within them when the Lord spoke: "Whom shall I send? And who will go for us?" (Isaiah 6:8). How amazing that the Almighty should be speaking to us, that He would stoop to give us a part in working for His kingdom.

"Here am I. Send me!" Isaiah had simply replied. This was the response of many of the Buhid who had glimpsed the glory of the Lord, the one look that truly opens eyes, and forever alters our perception of all things. They had glimpsed the pure dazzle of His radiance, whose piercing brilliance causes to fade and pale into insignificance the former bright things of this world. O the majesty of His being, whose presence graces the poor and humble lives of men and women who place their hope in Him, who fix their eyes on eternity and not on the passing riches that allure us today but are gone tomorrow.

CHAPTER FOURTEEN

OVERCOMING

Shortly before rising to lead worship in the Siyangi church, Oton, a young woman, came over to where Alexandra and I were sitting and put a message into my hand. She looked vaguely distraught and embarrassed, quickly returning to her place somewhere in the middle of the church. The note read: "I need to speak to you. Aynom wants to leave me!"

Aynom was her husband of only about three years. They had had one child but she had died when only a year old. They had not been able to conceive since.

After the service, Oton was lingering by the door and as we came to her, she pleaded:

"Help Aynom and myself! He is threatening to leave me. If you can speak God's word to us, then maybe there is a chance to sort things out!" We assured her that we would try to help but first we wanted to find a church elder to come with us. As it so turned out we had two church elders who accompanied us to the couple's house straight after the worship meeting. One was the gifted evangelist Buhadan (of the fangablang spirit fame) and the other was Marrangat, who, getting wind of what was being discussed, invited himself along, something we were not entirely happy with at this initial stage since he was Oton's father.

We gathered in the inner, more private room of the couple's house. The couple sat next to each other, looking very young and shy and understandably anxious. They had both known us for quite some time and this must have been a decisive factor in their asking us for help. After praying, we asked Aynom to explain why he wanted to leave Oton. This is was what he said:

"Our problems began when our daughter died. We were on a trip coming back from Calapan and the child had got very sick. Probably an aswang had bitten her on our travels, for she was not sick for long but died before we even got home.

"Later I searched my heart as to why this had happened and it came to mind that I had looked at a pretty girl lustfully. I confessed this to Oton and she started to beat me up, punching me all over in a fit of rage!"

"Did you hit her back?" I asked.

"No!"

"I would have got really angry if he had hit me back," Oton interjected. Her widened eyes gave me no reason to think that she would not have been true to her word. I admired Aynom's self-control for he was, like nearly all Buhid men, strong in the arm.

"Can we just get this clear," spoke Alexandra, "did Aynom only look at this pretty girl with lustful thoughts or did he go further than that with her?"

"I only looked and sinned in my mind!"

"And it was that that killed our child," added Oton with a sense of finality.

We investigated further to see if there were other significant factors. Whilst there was much talking and a good amount of cultural information the elders were eager to convey, the matter was not complex. Oton blamed Aynom for the death of their child. He had looked at this other woman and as a consequence, God punished them by sending an aswang along to bite their only child! Here the pagan mindset, coloured somewhat by a Christian complexion, was interpreting events to disastrous effect. As a result, Aynom had not only been chastised, but was under continued blame for the death of their child. Under the constant insinuations, he wanted to leave Oton.

They both looked to God to resolve their present impasse and needed to grasp that our Lord is not the cruel and vindictive God they mistook Him for, rather one who may exercise discipline but who is loving and forgiving, who has good plans for His people. It was the Mangyan's former lords who were capricious and behaved vengefully. Once this was established, we talked about confession to the Lord and God's forgiveness in connection with Aynom's "lustful look".

Oton was looking somewhat pleased with the progress of events until we reminded her of the need to respect her husband. We explained that it was not mature to leap to a pagan conclusion as to the cause of the child's death, and beat Aynom up. We read together the Lord's commands to husbands and wives in Ephesians five, drew out the principles and discussed ways in which these might be applied in the Buhid context. Oton recognised her need

to respect Aynom as the head of the house, and we acknowledged
the difficulty Oton faced, since she had been a Christian for a much
longer time than Aynom (although to judge by her interpretation
of events one wondered how much biblical teaching had really penetrated). Aynom was still shy of praying, whilst Oton was prac-
tised. Aynom had only recently become literate, whereas Oton was
a teacher of literacy.

There was certainly much disparity that required sensitivity.
Able to draw from our own experience, since I had become a
Christian some years after Alexandra had, we could identify with
Aynom's struggles to become the spiritual head of the household.
Alexandra shared with Oton the need to be humble, to hold back
in order to allow Aynom to assert his proper place in the home. We
applauded Aynom's honesty and heart-searching, for recognising
what biblically was indeed a sin, though no pagan Buhid would
ever have regarded it as such. We recommended that in confessing
lustful thoughts, it was best to do so primarily to the Lord, especially if the wife has a jealous and suspicious nature.

The outcome came much sooner than any of us had expected.
Oton asked Aynom's forgiveness, apologising for beating him up
and for wrongfully blaming him for the death of their child.
Aynom responded by forgiving her and asking her forgiveness for
wanting to walk out on her. The couple spontaneously touched
each other's arm in a natural gesture of reconciliation and Oton's
father prayed for them. All along he had very sensibly never shown
any favouritism towards his own daughter. Buhadan was surprised
how quickly all was resolved, remarking that Buhid had a high
respect for the advice of their missionaries. I felt sad that a similar
esteem was not offered to their own church elders.

The couple stayed together. Aynom grew in the Lord, and Oton
respected him for this. A new phase in their relationship had
begun, strengthened now for having overcome the problem
together and more committed to working at their marriage. Their
one sorrow was their inability to conceive a child for a long time.
They adopted Oton's youngest sister, who was more or less the

same age as the one child they had lost and, two years later, Oton proudly confided that she was expecting again.

This had been our first call to help counsel Buhid couples. We became aware of the sort of tensions arising in Buhid marriages. There was a low regard for the marriage bond, which, combined with the infidelity carried over from their pagan background, made us appreciate why Christian marriages were under considerable threat. This resulted in a far greater number of marital break-downs than in other Mangyan tribes whose pagan background looked dimly upon adultery.

This prompted a marriage seminar, specifically identifying the tensions and how to apply God's word. Such tensions included the interference of parents who thought nothing of trying to separate a daughter from a husband they regarded as lazy or sickly; the wife's transfer of affection from husband to child and the subse-quent neglect of her appearance; or the husband not being mindful of the need to help out in the home at times. These problems were by no means endemic throughout every marriage. A good number were fine models of Christian values whom others looked to for inspiration.

The infidelity issue though proved to be the Achilles' heel of the Buhid Church, and it was more often the wife who was the unfaith-ful partner, sometimes wanting to revert to the former custom of having two husbands. If the wife was attracted to a second man, yet found no particular fault with her first husband, then rather than separate, she would arrange for the two men to share her as their joint wife and live under one roof! The woman most often was the one who set out to attract another mate, and the men usually showed little resistance in succumbing to her charms. Married men were strangely exonerated by their wives, the wife blaming the other woman for tempting and luring her husband away.

It was no surprise that the Buhid elders had specifically prayed for a missionary family and not for a single man or woman. They hoped a couple might better understand the tensions and temptations that many Buhid marriages faced. That would not necessarily always be the case, and some couples might have been even stricter and less understanding than a single person would have been, if the single missionary could exercise imagination and humbly recognise their own human frailty in this regard.

Maybe we were particularly suited for this role though. We had had to face up to significant pressures upon our own marriage and had learned of the need to be committed to working things out. Once, we had seemed always to be at loggerheads, frequently misunderstanding the motives of the other. These pressures had really become apparent when we first arrived in the Philippines, and we felt exceptionally unworthy to be missionaries. A long time passed before we noticed that we had a basic interpretation problem as to whatever the other was saying. It was longer still before we learnt the need to repeat our understanding of what the other had just said, to avoid becoming embroiled in yet another argument. If we had been aware of this fact much sooner, we could have avoided much unnecessary tension.

There was another significant factor too. Many missionaries have to deal with marital difficulties, which frequently flare up on entering a new country and starting a new occupation, with all of the associated changes and inconveniences and extreme fatigue imposed by a different culture. The electricity was more frequently off than on, cutting off without warning, leaving us with no idea as to whether it would be just a short two- to four-hour cut, or a more lengthy one, which commonly lasted eight to sixteen hours in duration, sometimes even going on for two days! Stiflingly hot inside concrete houses constructed with small windows and tin roofs, electric fans are much needed. Our tempers therefore were unsurprisingly short. Add to this the tensions of learning a new language with such a vastly different grammar to European languages, of understanding an oriental culture and of trying to meet the needs and expectations of two young children bullied by our neighbour's wife. With interrupted sleep patterns and frequent fevers, it is no wonder that the pressures mounted.

But taking all this into account, there was yet another factor. Was not the arrival of a missionary family going to be contested by the devil himself? Slow in recognising this, it was only when we began to pray seriously together as man and wife against the ploys of the wily one that we began to notice a significant improvement. When we began to start misinterpreting the other we learned to stop and pray. Often only then did we begin to hear what the other was saying and to realise the good motives that often lay behind our spouse's words and behaviour.

We were subjected to ghoulish goings-on: doors violently slamming on windless nights, locked doors being frantically shaken, handles turning when upon investigation both our children were fast asleep. One night Alexandra and I woke up simultaneously to find our bed being brutally shaken. We had thought it was an earthquake until we realised that nothing else in the room was being disturbed. Then the bed rose a foot off the floor descending abruptly with a crash when we called out to the Lord. All was then still.

We removed the idol shelf on the staircase. Even though without idols, it was still a pagan altar and had been used beforehand. The majority of houses being built by lowland Filipino builders in the Philippines are consecrated by the sacrificial blood of a chicken and the burial of a paper talisman inscribed in Latin in the cement foundations. We called on like-minded missionaries to come and pray and to dedicate our house to the Lord, a consecration that we repeated in all our rented houses. Some missionaries ignore all this and maybe we would have been inclined to do so too had we not felt jinxed. But in all of this, God was preparing us, allowing us to pass through the fire in order to take the Buhid pagan fears seriously, recognising the divisiveness of Satan, especially where it matters and hurts most, within the covenant of marriage.

With eyes opened to the ploys of the devil, together with our increasing commitment to pray together, we moved on from miserable defeat to knowing the strong arm of the Lord upon us.

"Do not be anxious about anything, but in everything, by prayer and petition, with thanksgiving, present your requests to God. And the peace of God, which transcends all understanding will guard your hearts and your minds in Christ Jesus." (Philippians 4:6–7)

What we had encountered, the first rot setting into a marriage, the lack of commitment to love, the erosion of trust, the withering of hope, was so relevant to many Buhid couples. Quite a few couples asked us for counsel and prayer, knowing that we had been there and were sympathetic, and were not glib concerning the remedy.

When Alexandra was no longer able to come into the hills with me and counselling was still sought, this made it awkward. More often than not, it was the wife who first acknowledged marital problems and was looking for a sympathetic ear. It called for much discretion, and I opted to do the major part of the counselling when both parties were present, or failing that, would look for a third party to be present who was acceptable to the one seeking counsel. I faithfully tried to represent the woman's point of view as I had learned it from Alexandra. One of the practical pieces of advice she had often passed on had been to encourage the wife to focus on the positives in her man, few though they might be, and not be blinded to these by his extraordinary number of faults! This proved a great antidote for many husbands as well. In stressing the need to look for what is good in the other, it is also spiritually important to thank God for those good qualities, to affirm your mate in these, and always to attribute the best of motives when your spouse's words or actions are ambiguous.

"Finally, brothers, whatever is true, whatever is noble, whatever is right, whatever is pure, whatever is lovely, whatever is admirable – if anything is excellent or praiseworthy – think about such things." (Philippians 4:8)

Even if our counsel in all these matters matrimonial and otherwise was not entirely appropriate for their culture or situation, the Buhid knew we were keen to help and to encourage. They were always very accommodating, forgiving our shortcomings because they knew we loved them, bearing out the saying: "love covers over a multitude of sins" (I Pet. 4:8). A commitment to love is far more appropriate than being an anthropological expert when seeking to meet the deep needs of the community, although ideally, to have the two would be best. Asians are generally far more discerning about people than Westerners, probably due to the high premium they place on working at smooth relationships. Generally more skilled at reading someone's feelings and thoughts, they know if they are loved and valued. They confide in those who are genuinely sympathetic, whatever their qualifications. Being a missionary does not automatically provide the missionary with counselling skills.

Counselling has to go beyond mere listening. If effort is not made to empathise, you cease to relate. More than Westerners, Asians will expect the counsellor to propose solutions that will be readily acted upon. It is vital to be biblical in these proposals, and prayerful in their outworking, as the community invests such authority in the missionary. Therefore how necessary it is to distinguish, as Paul does, between what the Lord says and what you suggest (1 Cor. 7:12), and letting this difference be known.

We tried to learn from the Buhid. Often we were reluctant to state our point of view, wanting first to be informed before making any judgement. In spite of this, we did sometimes jump to premature conclusions, and thankfully the Buhid, feeling comfortable enough with us, pointed out that we had perhaps overlooked a certain matter or had not properly understood their "rather poor explanation" as they would humbly put it. How much easier it is to move forward and reach reconciliation when pride is not at stake.

The Buhid did hold their missionaries, our predecessors and ourselves alike, in tremendous esteem. I had to be particularly careful when making a flippant remark, or a light-hearted comment, that it was not taken in earnest and held as biblical truth. In a way, whatever I said "from the front" (the pulpit) was regarded rather as when the Pope speaks "ex cathedra". It taught me to be guarded with my tongue and to be quick to own up to any error I was aware of having made in my Bible exposition. When necessary, I made allusion to a point I had inaccurately made on a previous trip, or expanded upon something previously poorly stated. I continually emphasised the importance of testing every teacher's words with the authority of scripture, knowing there were already others coming to try to win them over to their denomination.

It was a fine line to walk. On the one hand it was necessary to answer their spiritual questions in as full a way as possible (recognising that they did not have recourse to any research materials), and yet at the same time, owning up to my own limited understanding, to the occasional silence of scripture or to the finiteness of the human mind. Since many of their questions would go way beyond the scope of the theme and texts under study, I sometimes found myself in uncharted waters concerning matters I had not properly explored in my reading of scripture. How necessary it was to distinguish between the things I was certain of, backed up by appropriate scripture references, and what I was unsure about, when I would emphasise that I was only offering a personal opinion or a partial understanding deserving further study. If it concerned an issue that touched several of them, then I took it as my cue to prepare a course of study on that topic and others relating to it. I learned to accept this quizzing, as sometimes being the prompting of the Holy Spirit.

Whatever we can contribute is minimal compared with the mighty arm of the Lord who is able to transform a difficult situation.

Once, in Apnagan, the church of the many able teachers, I was made aware of a case of adultery, involving Christians, which was upsetting the community. But its far-reaching ramifications were unknown to me. I was preaching through a series of sermons on the first ten chapters of Joshua, drawing out the principles of a consecrated life being vital in realising spiritual victory. I had reached the seventh chapter and was looking forward to preaching on this text.

Since waking up that Sunday morning I had been troubled in spirit about what I had to share. I had re-read my sermon notes a couple of times, each time satisfying myself that the preparation was sound and appropriate, and yet, minutes later, my spirit was uneasy once more. I went for a walk outside the village, to be alone with the Lord at a time when everyone was going off to Sunday school meetings preceding the worship service. I had no part in these meetings in Apnagan and so had the freedom of an hour to seek the Lord, to know if He wanted a different message from the one I had prepared.

Although I sensed God was wanting me to abandon my prepared message, I had no idea as to what I should preach upon instead. I flicked through the pages of a Bible I had brought along with me, debated various passages with myself, but without clear conviction. Uneasily, I tried to dismiss the issue, attributing the discomfort to my own making, to too much coffee and not enough sleep, and to having come to the end of yet another full week of intensive teaching. Once again I had been away from Alexandra and had had to deal with some heavy pastoral issues, which probably accounted for feeling ill at ease and jittery.

However much I tried to rationalise, my spirit remained ill at ease, providing no clue as to what was required. Even sustained prayer and waiting in silent expectation did nothing to alleviate the way I was feeling. I was convinced that the Lord was requiring something else from me during the worship service, which by now was fast approaching.

The iron girder outside the church was struck, and still perplexed, I entered the building. I put aside the sermon notes but reread the seventh chapter of Joshua. The text struck me afresh as being very appropriate. Its key message was very clear. If a church deliberately ignores God's command, how could God's people walk on in victory? Achan knew the command to consecrate all the plundered treasure to the Lord, and so in hiding a little, he was not only disregarding God's will, but also rejecting His Lordship.

The parallel became clear with the Apnagan situation. How could the Apnagan church move on in victory and in fellowship with God, if two of its members had fallen into adultery? I argued it was only two people who had fallen into sin and that the rest of the church seemed appalled by what they had done. The Spirit reminded me that it was only Achan who had concealed the forbidden treasure – yet this individual defiance had ramifications for the whole community!

I was called up to the front to share "the word of the Lord", a timely reminder that it was indeed God's message and not my own. I called everyone to turn with me to Joshua chapter seven. At least that much was clear. I chose someone with a strong, clear voice to read it out from the front. Whilst those verses were being read, so familiar to my ears, I was now particularly impressed by verse twelve:

> "That is why the Israelites cannot stand against their enemies; they turn their backs and run because they have been made liable to destruction. **I will not be with you any more unless you destroy whatever among you is devoted to destruction.**"

I had brought my sermon notes with me to the front and began speaking from the introduction I had prepared to this chapter. To have proceeded with those notes however would have been a wilful act of disobedience. I closed the notes and uncomfortably declared to the congregation that I was not very sure what the Lord would have me say this morning! That was a good line to make everyone sit up and take attention! Next I prayed. For once in my life, I was going to be truly led by the Spirit, having finally abandoned my preparations.

Afterwards, three things struck me about the sermon. First, it was the shortest I have ever preached. Secondly, everyone was really taking note as to what was being said. And thirdly, I was not at a loss for words, for I spoke with a fluency unusual for me even when speaking English!

Although this was an example of being led by the Spirit, I was not preaching on some totally unfamiliar text. I had studied this text from various angles and knew a fair amount of its import, since it was part of a series of sermons all based on Joshua. God still used all that research and insight, but demanded my dependence upon Him.

Whilst preaching, I was very conscious of the rapt attention of the whole church. People were not their often fidgety selves. The stillness extended to the children too! I don't know whether the children were present and quiet or had gone en masse with their antics elsewhere. Even the dogs were still or absent, as were the chickens within the church. No one had that glazed look, the spiritual veil that blinded them from seeing the truth, but all were on tenterhooks, anxious not to miss the point.

As I drew to a close, the Lord encouraged me to invite people forward to make a response to His message, to get themselves right with Him.

I inwardly groaned, appalled by the idea, for not only did I come from a very conservative church background that did not make challenges of this nature, but I had been warned, earlier in our time with the Buhid, never to invite this kind of response, as the Buhid, being exceptionally shy, would never step forward. I argued with the Lord that I couldn't do this, that it was inappropriate. I excused myself, hiding behind the reasoning that I was hearing perhaps another voice and not the Lord's. I inwardly pointed out to the Lord that I had already abandoned my own sermon and that now, what He was requiring, would result in me looking an utter fool. I did not wish to act against my own judgement.

The inner conviction came again. I was to trust Him just as I had trusted Him with the message.

So I did trust God. I called forward anyone challenged by the message, who needed to put themselves right with God before they left the church that morning. I then called forward anyone who wanted prayer for a health matter. These two reasons would give a sense of cover to those who needed to put right anything connected with adultery. I had cited this sin as one reason for spiritual dryness, for the Lord appearing to be far off.

I had not anticipated any response but knew better than to flagrantly disobey the Lord. Better to live with embarrassment over no one coming forward, than to go home knowing that I had wilfully disobeyed.

First one or two folk came forward, then a major move of what seemed like three-quarters of the congregation were suddenly up on their feet, waiting their turn at the front. A sound of sobbing filled the church. The strongest and the most reserved had tears running down their cheeks. The Buhid do not show these emotions publicly. Excessive displays of emotion embarrass them even at a funeral, although occasionally someone might surreptitiously wipe away a tear. In this they greatly differ from the Luktanon.

When just a few folk were coming forward, I called the elders to pray for those wanting to put themselves right with the Lord. I did not get involved at first because I felt this was something the church elders should handle. But one of the young elders called me over to counsel someone with a problem beyond his ken. With the great surge forward, it would have been inappropriate for me to remain aloof from the prayer counselling. I was particularly struck by the general sense of desperation as those who had come to the front made confession.

Before that service, I had only seen part of the picture, was only aware of part of the problem in Apnagan at that time. The adulterous relationship I mentioned earlier had apparently caused all sort of rumours to abound and insinuations to be made, implicating a great number in the community. More seriously, since a couple of Christians had openly flaunted their unholy union, other Christians were tempted to flirt with another's spouse.

Some were there at the front in response to the need for healing. They were prayed for and many were healed of arthritis and nausea, recurrent headaches and ulcers. But not all were healed. Personally, my faith was challenged when Lukmoy, a man crippled by polio, came forward, piteously walking upon his haunches. I prayed for him, all the while wrestling and lamenting over my unbelief that he would be healed. It was not the question of whether God could, but rather would, He heal?

Lukmoy returned home just as crippled. He also left with a stubborn heart, a spirit too scared to confess his complicity with the adulterous couple in providing his home as their love nest. This was not known by others at the time, but was revealed in subsequent weeks when he duly repented. Onan, the old man so crippled with arthritis and conveyed to the church in the back of another's sledge, was also among those whom the Lord chose not to relieve. But Onan returned unshaken in his faith, with the serenity of one at peace with God, longing for the day when he would shuffle off the pains of the body and receive a new body in the coming age.

As folk confessed and received the forgiveness of the Lord and returned to their seats, while many more were still up front waiting their turn in the aisle, I encouraged one of the girls who often led worship to lead us in praising God. This also prevented eavesdropping. The worship leader gathered a few around her and began to sing. Others soon took up the refrain and began to sing with a sincerity I had not often heard before, rendered with a beauty that was not of this world. The singing was indeed heavenly, naturally welling up into praise and worship from the heart, in celebration of a new-found communion with the Lord of Hosts.

I have sometimes doubted my suitability for heaven, reflecting upon my apprehension over continually singing praises to the Lord. I have not always enjoyed singing hymns; nor am I often in raptures about the latest worship song. I am not particularly fond of the organ, and in all honesty I greatly prefer classical pieces to much of the sacred music. But if what I experienced for half an hour in that church on top of a muddy hilltop out in the South China Sea is anything to go by, I will enjoy heaven and will not tire of singing God's praise, nor be impatient to get out and do something else. I will have new ears to appreciate worship and a clean heart along with everyone else, to sing God's praises. What is more, I will not want to stop singing my great Redeemer's praise just as it was that Sunday morning. I was so very reluctant to stop. The whole church, with one voice and one devotion, offered our hearts before the throne of Him who loves us.

What a transformation: from God declaring: "I will not be with you any more" to being caught up in unison in singing His praises. We had met with Him and received His forgiveness and healing.

What perplexes me though was why did this time of brief revival not tarry? I visited folk that afternoon and many were still talking about what had happened, testifying to being healed of various ailments, but come the evening service, the wonder had quite gone, the memory put to rest as the old routine was re-established. There was no sense of expectation, no declaration of having met with the Holy One.

This saddened and disturbed me. No report of what had clearly taken place went out to the other Buhid churches. I still find myself asking why could that be? How could a people, confronted by an indignant Lord, who had made confession, received forgiveness, and known the Spirit of the Lord come upon them – how could they go away forgetting what had taken place?

I was changed by that experience. I realise that we cannot so much call down blessing on our preparations, but rather need to acknowledge, more than ever, our need to be led by the Lord, of being prepared to go beyond our comfort zone, beyond any previous experience or expectation, and come to trust and rely on Him to perform more than we would ever imagine.

CHAPTER FIFTEEN

GOING HOME

"Faduwasay – we want to say that we look forward to your coming back," remarked Sayna, looking hesitant. "But maybe you will decide that it is too difficult to come back to living with us here in our muddy hills; you may decide that it is so good to be back at home among your own people and so remain with them!"

"No. God willing, we shall be back next year, at the start of the new rainy season!" I replied. "You know there is nothing that I would like better than to be back with you all again."

Sayna let go a brief salvo of laughter. Another listening in let out a small whoop of delight. Sayna remarked: "That will be good and we can hear more of our Father's words. We hope that you will come to Safang Uyang again, even though we are the least of all the Buhid churches?" By now, Sayna had sidled up so close that not only were our shoulders touching, but he deliberately lent some of his weight upon me.

"Don't put yourselves down too much for being the smallest," I replied. "Remember Gideon – he came from the weakest clan of their tribe and considered himself the least in his family and look how he was chosen by God!"

Sayna lent away thoughtfully, smiled, then lent his weight back on me again. He nodded his head in assent. Looking at his watch, from which he was never parted, he announced in a loud voice to those hanging around near the church: "It's time to start again!"

Apnagan was hosting the Buhid church conference. It was notable on a couple of counts. Firstly, the Safang Uyang church had come en masse and six of their number were to be baptised that weekend. We lingered in one another's presence, experiencing again that wonderful fellowship, that foretaste of heaven we had all known on my single trip to their small village.

The other notable feature was the presence of five young men who had come right across the dividing, central mountain chain from the far coast. Two days they had been on the trail, and three of them were not Christian. They came from the small village of Datag Bonglay – the church that had never grown, in a community deeply divided between two clans. The presence of these five was significant for no one had come from Datag Bonglay in recent years to these conferences. Their coming was like a first ripple, preceding a wave that would sweep through that divided community.

Some months after this conference, those much-prayed-for Christians in Datag Bonglay reported a number turning to the Lord, and requested help not only in the building of a larger church, but also in discipling the many who were young in the faith. The church building there was indeed very small, like a large garden shed, with short benches for three abreast, and was quite unable to accommodate all the new believers who jostled for position at the front and side doors, once there was no further room for another soul to squeeze into the mêlée within. The church was much relieved by a work party who came over the central mountains to build a much larger church as well as taking the opportunity to teach God's word.

The conference meetings ran from eight in the morning till late at night. The evening sessions created an animated throng of bodies all squashed up together under the heat and glare of three pressure lanterns hoarsely howling away on the roof beams. Despite the cool evening, the close-packed quarters made everyone run with sweat and the atmosphere became high in more senses than one! The evening meetings were lengthy for this was the time when folk liked to perform "special numbers".

Apnagan was home to those who delighted to sing to the Lord, who wrote their own hymns and worked hard at perfecting their worship. They were in demand throughout the whole island to lead "worship seminars" and formed two teams to meet these requests.

This last conference reminded me of the first Mangyan conference we had attended, not with the Buhid, but with the tribe to the north – the Tawbuid. It had been held one Easter and had sealed our calling to the Mangyan. Even back then a rapport was established, a special fellowship we had not known during the years spent in the Luktanon churches, a particular thoughtfulness they showed that was not lost on us. Someone, unbidden, had brought a pile of firewood to the house we were staying in, another a neatly tied bundle of freshly-picked sweet potato leaves to stew, all given at a time when they were literally inundated by hundreds of visitors from other villages and tribes disrupting the peace of their village routine.

I recall how we had misunderstood the time of the sunrise service to be held on Easter morning and how Alexandra and I had gone along to the church at something like four-thirty in the morning, only to find it full of sleeping forms who had nowhere else to sleep in this small tribal village. But that early-morning mistake proved to be an appointment with the Lord. We looked out upon the sheer splendour of the full moon hanging low in the western sky. The bright moonlight left a glittering track upon the South China Seas, captivating our hearts and enthralling the eye.

The dark, still water, seen at night, did not seem far off, for the mountain fell steeply away, down towards the sea. We sat down upon a large rock some height above the church, quietly drinking in this holy scene. The moon was like a floodlight, bright upon the cogon roof of the church, yet under the substantial eaves, the rest of the structure was in shadow. The lighter mass of the calm waters way down below, yet seeming so close, formed the perfect backdrop to this rustic church etched in silhouette upon the silvery sea. It was so peaceful. Not even the cockerels stirred and the silver light fell prolifically in certain places, on particular forms, not only on the roofs, but on the motionless fronds of the banana groves. We were the only ones in raptures, for not another soul roamed abroad at that hallowed hour.

There in Apnagan no special moonlight shone just for our benefit but the time was no less special. The blessing was not privately enjoyed alone on a mountainside in the hour before dawn, but was corporately felt as brothers and sisters in Christ experiencing the wonder of our oneness. It is not cultural for Buhid to hug, but the looks, the unsaid speech of the heart evident in lustrous eyes that no longer shyly averted when our eyes met, were unforgettable, warm embraces.

At the end of communion, all the men lined one side of the building and the women the other, with several smaller groups forming circles in between. At the command, we clasped hands and sang the communion song: "My Lord who redeemed me at Calvary", at the end of which, still holding hands, we joyfully raised our arms into the air with the final flourish of "My Lord" being raised a few decibels higher.

I urged them to stand by their elected elders and give them all the encouragement and support that they had shown us, as God is no respecter of nationalities. If they were to prosper and move forward with the Lord, they needed to realise that it is through surrender to God, not the leading of a foreign missionary that the church was going to advance. How important it was for the progress of the gospel, that the Buhid should identify the men and women of God's choosing, and humble themselves and unite under their spiritual leadership. The obstacle to this, we discovered, was that the Buhid formed a classless society, without social hierarchy, making them question why they should serve under one of their own kind.

During typhoon season, when a deluge can fall from the heavens for four to five days incessantly, there rises such a flood in the rivers that the broad stony valleys become a roaring torrent of rich, murky brown waters, sweeping away banana palms, sometimes whole trees and houses built foolishly upon the flood plains. With a sustained assault of this kind on many of the unstable bridges, the man-made structures come tumbling down, seriously disrupting communications and the traffic of people and goods.

Such was the condition of the Buhid Church we had found four years before, surviving but cut off, introspective, having lost its commerce with the people on the other side of the river, the lost of their own tribe. The bridge that at one time spanned the river needed rebuilding; the concrete slabs used to erect a secure structure, were the word of God. The bridge had required many such slabs to span the whole extent. The slabs were not easy to haul about and position into place, but required a crane to raise and then to lower them into their correct place. The crane was an effective servant, one who was consecrated to the task concerning the honour of the Lord who commissioned the bridge to be erected. Sometimes the stretch to correctly position a slab was uncommonly far, requiring a reach beyond the normal procedure, necessitating the jib arm to be extended. Such tricky manoeuvres required the prayer of faith, which like that fully extended jib arm, reached beyond the usual span of activity.

Our second missionary term had come to an end and God had rebuilt his bridge. We were no more than the crane, a servant used for a time. The purpose was to span the gap, to mobilise the Church and enable them to cross to the regions beyond their locality, with the most important message of all time. The bridge had been reconstructed through prayer and Bible teaching. The many baptisms that came out of this encouraged these believers to pass over the waters in victory, beyond their fears of the flood, and made them keen to tell their stories, of how they had been liberated, to those living on the other side. The Church had been mobilised, not where we would have determined, among the Bangon, but according to the sovereign will of God. " 'For my thoughts are not your thoughts, neither are your ways my ways,' declares the Lord."

There is a sense of failure. The Bangon sub-tribe we had envisaged reaching with the gospel remained unreached with the exception of the occasional individual. We came to acknowledge that before another people can be reached, the existing Church near to hand must first be transformed. Without renewal they will never have the passion to speak of the glory of God to others living under fear.

What is a vision if others do not have a passion for it? And how can there be a passion if there is not first a sense of longing for God? How can there be desire without first glimpsing the beauty of Christ?

"Come, all you who are thirsty, come to the waters."

And was there a thirst? His word rained on parched ground, watering the dust, making it flourish and bud. The Buhid didn't remain out in the parched wilderness, but came to the waters and plunged into newness of life, going "out with joy" and being "led forth with peace".

It is the Lord who should rightfully direct. When the breath of His Holy Spirit awakens the sleeper, and the Church gives fully of herself, our fine sounding vision statements and logical strategies sometimes have to be put aside. Gladly I let my vision be consumed in the heaven-sent fire that sets aflame a man's heart.

As missionaries, we failed ever to become truly proficient in the Buhid language, feeling only comfortable in using it conversationally, fearing that our insufficient grasp might lead our hearers astray, or frustrate them in their desire to know God. With the exception of teaching at the Safang Uyang church where the Lord wonderfully enabled me to explain spiritual truths in Buhid since some could not understand Tagalog very well, I taught almost exclusively in the Tagalog language, the trade language of Mindoro and a substantial part of the Philippines. This would perhaps be considered more a problem by linguistically able people than it ever was to the Buhid themselves, who, although preferring us to teach in their heart language, obviously still profited from the Tagalog medium. We are not proud of this linguistic shortcoming, still feeling ashamed that we did not become fluent, but God was glorified nonetheless. I believe it underlines an important principle: God can use imperfect communication. Our interaction is not by language alone, but through the sharing of our lives, through being wholly committed to loving the people God leads us to, dependent upon the Lord and wholeheartedly committed to prayer.

We always had a transient status. We were "on loan" to the Buhid for a short time, a brief period to understand a specific tribal culture, before moving on into a wider itinerant ministry among some of the other Mangyan tribal churches. We had put it to the Buhid elders, that in view of this short time, would they prefer us either to major in learning their language or in teaching the word of God in Tagalog? They replied resoundingly with one voice for the latter.

It was the better choice, but not without many frustrations, for we did not always follow their discussions in Buhid. We had many notebooks full of Buhid words, phrases and texts that we busily scribbled down when visiting folk, with every good intention of analysing and committing them to memory during our sparse spare time, but regrettably this was not always our practice.

One former missionary, who became a valued prayer warrior for us and for the Buhid, remarked that our brief ministry of three-and-a-half years among the Buhid (preceded by three-and-a-half years of preparation in the lowlands) was characterised by a sense of urgency, a wholehearted commitment to teaching God's word and to disciple His people.

"Preach the word; be prepared in season and out of season; correct, rebuke and encourage – with great patience and careful instruction." (2 Timothy 4:2)

The Lord had called us by that verse seven years earlier whilst we were making our first ascent to the tribal village of Ayan Bekeg upon the mighty slopes of Mount Halcon. A focus on the word of God characterised our time there – exposing the false teaching of the cults which prowled around the scraps of the Church like ravenous wolves; correcting patterns of unchristian behaviour that consumed like a cancer from within and ushered back the dark realm of pagan culture; stressing the supremacy of Christ in overcoming any terror.

Better to see our man-made, finite plans fail through God overriding these, than see them realised through human ingenuity and tenacity alone and look upon some spiritless edifice that becomes defunct upon our leaving.

Our plans for a third term of service were abruptly shattered. Many issues obstructed our return: the appropriate grade placement between Scottish and American secondary school systems proved highly problematic, and this, with Iain's unhappy dorm experience, as well as my health issues, led OMF to advise us strongly not to return.

God though is not taken by surprise.

The final banquet was eagerly anticipated, but before this was served, the one Buhid leader who had never really accepted me made me a farewell speech. He testified to how the Lord was strengthening the churches, the first of many testimonies I would hear over the final weeks as I went from church to church. But now it was banquet time, the culmination of the gathering in Apnagan. During, the previous night, four or five pigs had been slaughtered, and the entire night had been spent butchering and preparing for this feast. Two huge sacks of rice had been carried up at the commencement of the conference and shared out between households to be cooked in every available pan and turned out onto banana leaves laid across the church benches. The pork meat cooked in large woks with no flavourings was just stewed in water, plain chunks of pork, some on the bone, others with huge chunks of fat that sometimes came with the outer bristle of the hog. This stew was poured into plastic buckets, which the elders carried around the crowd, ladling portions out onto mounds of rice as people eagerly held out their plates. This rare treat was relished with much smacking of lips.

That night, the concluding part of the conference, was an affair that started and continued as it meant to go on, with much praise to the Lord. Individuals and groups came without break to sing their piece from the front. They seemed intent to be still singing at dawn the following day.

Isaias, a man in his mid-twenties, rose to his feet.

"'Going Home!'" someone shouted out. Another whooped with delight, inspiring a whole chorus of whoops and whistles. "Going Home" was a song Isaias sang without fail on the last evening of every conference, always greeted with much cheering. Isaias picked his way over legs and sleeping dogs, making his way to the front.

"This one is especially for our faduwasay!" Isaias spotted me in the sea of faces, his sparkling eyes narrowed into the most benevolent of grins. The Buhid had correctly predicted what the song was going to be before Isaias had started singing, for it was in truth the only song he ever sang from the front as a solo and no one else ever sang it – it was regarded as Isaias' song!

The crowd were in raptures as Isaias had an excellent voice, full and emotive. Whilst he sang the chorus, he pretended to wipe away tears, included my name in every chorus line, looking me straight in the face all the while. His eyes shone not with tears, but full of his good nature welling up and overflowing from within him. Isaias may have been no preacher, but he was full of love for his fellow man, endowed with a loving charisma and an infectious laugh. Too few churches are gifted with such a personality, a man who makes a difference, whose absence is sorely apparent. Heaven will be that more special because of his presence.

CHAPTER SIXTEEN

A GREAT LEAP FORWARD

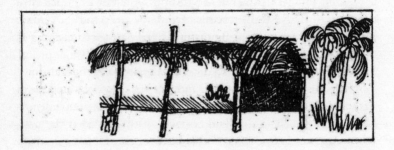

"Father – may the chant of the shamen be blown away by the wind that it may not be heard, or if it is heard, may it be impossible for the demon spirits to do anything. Lord – reveal yourself to this people so they may know your salvation and come to acknowledge you their Maker and their Saviour."

Buhadan was praying alone late at night, a lone Christian in the pagan stronghold of Fontan. The evangelist was not the only one awake at that late hour, for he was only too aware of the three shamen about their monotonous chant. For the best part of the evening they had been interceding with the spirits of the dead on behalf of the greater part of the community who had come down with high fevers.

Buhadan could not rest. It was not so much the constant chant droning on just a couple of houses away that prevented him from sleeping, but rather the oppressive atmosphere that weighed heavily upon his soul, as the shamen sought contact with the realm of evil. Above all, though, Buhadan was there for the purpose of the Kingdom of God, anxious to see a breakthrough in this resistant place. This was just one of many visits. He longed to see the people of Fontan coming to know the Lord. They were interested to listen to his explanations about the Lord who created them, they pointed to his coloured pictures to clarify his explanations, and asked questions revealing true interest. Yet in spite of all these encouraging indications, the people were holding back. They could not bring themselves to believe, they were just not sure that the God of Buhadan was the Lord Almighty who was greater still than the sum total of the forces of evil. How could they be certain Buhadan spoke the truth? By turning to Christ, they truly risked the full retribution of the demon spirits.

Now this sickness had descended upon most of the Fontan community. Those who had shown an interest in the gospel were almost without exception afflicted by the sickness, either personally, or through another within their household. This was clearly retribution indeed, inflicted by their ancestral spirits because the living had dared show an interest in the Creator God. Who was going to care for the needs of the dead ancestors should they all turn to the Lord? The spirits were angry, the villagers reasoned, and had sent this sickness as a reminder that they were not to be thrown over. They were asserting themselves as the lords of the earth.

The frantic squeals of a pig, cornered at a nearby house by a group of three men, brought Buhadan to the door. One was armed with a heavy, thick branch, which he swung with great alacrity and accuracy, stunning the boar, knocking it from its feet. The two other men immediately set to, one straddling the pig's back to ensure it was pinned to the ground whilst the other swooped down by the beast's head. Grabbing the boar by an ear he jerked back the head and ran his newly sharpened fotol blade right across the exposed throat, cutting clean through the windpipe and jugular. The slaughter was quickly performed. They trussed the pig up with vine and suspended it from a horizontal pole placed between two houses so they could butcher the carcass. Two more pigs were soon slaughtered in similar manner and the night was passed preparing the grim offerings to the spirits of the dead.

The last of the chickens in Fontan had been slaughtered the previous night, but the fever had not abated. The spirits were demanding a greater sacrifice, said the shamen, otherwise they would not have taken the child who had died last night! Fear and foreboding gripped the entire community. Buhadan had become the outcast, the reason for this demand for greater blood sacrifices. Had he not come and lured them with his fascinating stories, to which they had unwisely listened? Had they not come close to believing in the Creator God?

No one slept that night. All able hands were busy preparing the cooked meat offering to appease the anger of the spirits. The shamen kept up their night-long chant, never wearying, but rather becoming more animated, almost into a state of possession. Fires burned, water was fetched, axes were busy chopping wood for the devouring flames, and blackened cooking pots were suspended over the fires as the sacrifice was prepared as best they knew how.

Buhadan was not idle through all of this time. Despite all those visits made up the Aliyanon River, over the central dividing range and on into the Occidental province to share the Good News, all the interest shown seemed now to be going up in smoke. From his home in Siyangi, it was a full day's walk there and back, but he had gladly walked all those hours, had given up those working days on his land, for the sake of seeing this community respond to the Lord. They had seemed so close! But now, watching those grim preparations, the villagers' conversion had never seemed so far away. All those who were capable were in some way engaged in the business of preparing the sacrifice for the demons.

"O Father," continued Buhadan, aloud to himself, but with a subdued tone, "reveal Yourself to these people that they may turn from these demon ways and worship the Living God. How can you stand by and watch these people suffer and not be touched by compassion for all those who are deceived by the spirits? Have pity on them, Lord, and rescue them not only from the grave that many imminently fear, but from the strong hands of the dark ones. Bare your mighty arm and deliver them from the tyranny of Satan, lead them through this thick darkness that so envelops them, and bring them into your marvellous light so they may see and taste that You are good!"

So Buhadan's prayer developed through the night. He had determined not to sleep, recognising that the Lord was far more worthy to be worshipped and praised than all these demons who kept the major part of the community awake and making sacrifice. Why should he not, the servant of the true God, pray and worship just as much as those shamen? Buhadan grew jealous for the honour of the Lord; his one all-consuming desire was to see the Lord magnified, honoured and lifted up in Fontan as He rightly should be, and his tribal brethren freed from the satanic clutch, free to serve the Almighty.

That night there was another death, this time not a child, but a mother. She had been sickly for some months, could not withstand the fever, and so breathed her last. Growing fear and panic was taking hold, for nothing seemed as if it could placate the wrath of the spirits. Many feared the ancestors were bent on the destruction of the entire village. The fevers were worsening, and one or two new folk, previously untouched by the epidemic, were now succumbing to its fiery grip.

Towards morning, as the thick darkness was yielding, Buhadan, who like Jacob had wrestled with the Lord all night long, began to articulate in his mind a feeling that had been growing all the while. It seemed that God was giving him a special gift of faith. The Lord was going to do something special in their midst, vindicate his servant, and raise His own honour like a standard in that pagan ground. The gift of faith is mentioned in 1 Corinthians 12, a passage about the gifts of the Spirit, and is obviously more than the common faith that every believer receives. It is a gift from God for a special purpose. God was going to answer Buhadan's prayers and the prayers of many saints in Siyangi and further afield.

The weary shamen suddenly appeared at Buhadan's door, their faces darkly drawn by sleeplessness and the diabolical grip of the demons. Realising their supplications had not only come to nought, but worse still had not prevented an adult from being claimed that night despite the killing of every chicken and the slaughter of the three pigs, they had reached a conclusion as to the obstacle.

"You have to go!" announced one of the shamen as Buhadan, emerging from his doorway, dropped to the ground beside them.

"Since you came into this village," began another, the most elderly of the three, "all our intercessions have been to no avail. The sacrifices have been unheeded. Our charms and amulets have no powers when you are around. When you pray to your God, the spirits refuse to do anything for us. The people say that your strange teaching has angered the ancestors. You are not wanted here, you are to leave this place this morning and never to come back again!"

The old man was about to turn and move off with his two companions when Buhadan spoke.

"The spirits have blinded you. Don't you see they have no power when I have come in the name of the Almighty Lord? This long night through you have chanted in vain to the spirits of the dead, and the fever is rife, hungry to devour another life no doubt before this day is through. Last night you shed sacrificial blood but God has already sent His Son as a sacrifice to cover over all our turning away from Him. Whoever puts his faith in the blood of Christ will please the Father – the Almighty One.

"The true Lord has spoken to me. Today you will see His mighty arm, powerful to deliver, to save you not only from the grip of this fever but also from the clutch of the demons. Today the Lord is going to do something new, something that you have never seen before. Today you will witness with your very own eyes, the salvation of the Lord who reigns.

"Come – let us go together into every household, and I will lay hands on the sick, and speak of my Lord to whom I will pray on their behalf."

The shamen after a moment's hesitation did not object. They were prepared to see which of the lords was the all-powerful One since all their efforts had produced nothing. Maybe Buhadan spoke truly and people would be healed? If he did not speak the truth, then they would expel him.

Together they went into the house that had received Buhadan and there he prayed for the sick, first explaining about the Christ in whose name he was going to pray. There were no visible manifestations of healing, but Buhadan did not feel perturbed. He knew this was not his own idea. No one objected to his prayers, for they were desperate and had given up any real hope of the demons delivering them. In this manner, trailed by his unlikely companions, the three shamen, Buhadan went from house to house, extolling the miraculous powers of Christ who called upon them to place their trust in Him and rid themselves once and for all of the tyranny of the demons. Again Buhadan placed his hands on all those who had fever and prayed simply and full of faith for their healing as well as for their believing.

By the time they had worked their way through every household and were leaving the last house in the village, they were met by a group of children.

"Aren't you one of the ones sick with fever just a while ago?" asked a shaman of one of the children. It quickly became apparent that the fever had abated. The previously sick were up and about, setting their houses in order. A couple of the children in the group confirmed that they too had been burning with fever just an hour earlier and now their bodies had been healed! As morning developed and the cooking fires sent smoke into the air, obscuring the burning sun, many of the healed were off in search of food and firewood to cook their first proper meal in three days.

Two of the three shamen believed and placed their trust in the God of Buhadan who now was being acclaimed, by all manner of people, as being the God of Fontan. But the third shaman would not believe, maintaining that the curse of sickness and death had been lifted by their night-long chanting and by the sacrifice of the pigs.

As much as the other two former shaman reasoned and argued, the third stubbornly denied, raising his voice and spitting on the ground before them as a sign of utter disgust – and his own blindness.

Fourteen households in all came to faith that day and gave thanks and worship to their new Lord. The two shamen gathered together their amulets, the highly prized, smooth, white stones worn about the waist in a pouch within a rattan belt, stones gathered from secret springs in the mountains, imbued with power from secret incantations, reinforced by the ritual sacrifice of chicken blood poured over them on every full moon. They took all these fetishes and burned those that could be destroyed by fire, shattered others that could be pounded to powder by the milling pole, and buried the remainder far from prying eyes so that these would not become a snare to future generations.

Within a few months, the believers of Fontan had united with the Christians of Balahok, half an hour's walk up river, by making new homes on land situated between their two villages. They called their new site Baliya. I refer to the place as "Baliya Fontan" as a testimony to what the Lord had done at Fontan, miraculously bringing this believing community into being.

Why do we not see God moving more often in miraculous ways?

This begs a question. If we have no experience, or worse still, no expectation of God of breaking through into our tough encounters with the pagan world, then is it not we who have changed, since the first century? God does not change: "Jesus Christ is the same yesterday and today and forever" (Hebrews 13:8). He still reveals Himself to those who look to Him in faith and call out to Him to transform a situation.

Buhadan was not seeking some thrilling experience of God for his own personal edification. He was not in search of the sensational. Rather, Buhadan was jealous for the honour of God. His motivation was to share Christ with his fellow people who lived in fear and submission to the capricious spirits. For the most excellent purpose of making the Good News known, God was keen to authenticate His servant's message.

Concerning this witness to the salvation from God, the writer to the Hebrews remarks:

"God also testified to it [salvation] by signs, wonders and various miracles, and gifts of the Holy Spirit distributed according to His will." (Hebrews 2:4)

Speaking of the impact made by Jesus' ministry, Peter spoke in a similar manner:

"Jesus of Nazareth was a man accredited by God to you by miracles, wonders and signs, which God did among you through him as you yourselves know." (Acts 2:22)

Paul's reliance was not on his very substantial intellect and considerable biblical knowledge, but rather on the Holy Spirit:

"I came to you in weakness and fear, and with much trembling. My message and my preaching were not with wise and persuasive words, but with a demonstration of the Spirit's power, so that your faith might not rest on men's wisdom, but on God's power." (1 Corinthians 2:3–5)

Likewise, miracles are often present when a faithful Christian steps into the pagan darkness with the gospel light and calls upon the Lord to reveal His glory. The Acts of the Apostles is sprinkled with such testimonies. The darkness is rent by the rising sun and the frontiers of the Kingdom are advanced, all for the glory of God.

Buhadan held onto God with a tenacity that would not let go until the Lord changed the situation. How many of us have ever really prayed like that? Willing to follow where God led him, regularly walking five hours upriver to share the Good News, losing material progress to keep pace with the majority of his tribal Christians. An adventurer in matters of faith, he stepped out beyond the familiar as a result of searching prayer. He dared to stake his own reputation (together with that of his Lord) when he laid hands on the sick and, having proclaimed the Good News, prayed for them with a childlike faith that God was pleased to answer. Have we ever had that openness and dared risk our reputation through such prayer? But we should not seek to do so until first we have met with God in prayer and the Spirit brings conviction. Such praying is born out of an inner confidence the Holy Spirit inspires within:

> "This is the confidence we have in approaching God: that if we ask anything according to His will, He hears us. And if we know that He hears us – whatever we ask – we know that we have what we asked of Him." (1 John 5:14–15)

I am pleased this happened to Buhadan and not to me, so that the villagers' confidence could truly rest upon the Lord and not upon the missionary. Interestingly, Buhadan's reaction to the miraculous events differed from mine. Although he was delighted about what had taken place, he was not astounded, for he had expected the miraculous to be revealed.

Were not all the hindrances of my limited health and the restrictions imposed by the NPA within God's plan to promote the Buhid believer and sideline the foreign missionary? Buhadan was an ordinary man through whom no sensational miracles had been performed before. Not one to boast of a healing ministry, he modestly went about His Father's business, declaring the way of salvation, the freedom from fear.

* * *

The Baliya Fontan church came into being at the time that the Buhid churches were still supporting Samwil and Ibilin. It posed the question of who was going to disciple this new church and how were they to be supported, considering the Buhid Church's difficulty in maintaining just one missionary couple?

We mentioned this matter as an item of prayer to our prayer partners. A couple of them wrote saying they would like to fund a second missionary couple to go to Baliya Fontan. We were sorely tempted (although we had never intended to solicit funds), yet significantly, in the Lord's timing, it had also been brought to our attention, both by first-hand example as well as through a document entitled "When the Mission Pays the Pastor", that foreign sponsorship is not always the great idea it first seems. The local church often "disowns" the mission when foreign finances are accepted. It is no longer theirs. The concern of caring for their own local missionary has become someone else's responsibility. Where the vision is lost, so is the prayer commitment, and without the informed prayer of the local church, the mission is greatly disadvantaged.

Rightly or wrongly we declined these two, kind, financial offers. But it did not solve the problem. There was not a couple prepared to uproot and abandon their fields without clear financial backing. The Buhid Church said that they couldn't support a second couple, even though, if every believing household in all of the Buhid churches increased their giving by just two pesos (the cost of an egg) a week, they could support not just one more missionary family, but two!

The problem was not just a matter of heart, of dedicated giving of a manageable amount by all. It was made worse by the distance between the churches and the lack of traffic between them. Furthermore cordial relations did not always exist between the villages.

To exacerbate the situation further, other denominations began showing a greater interest in the Mangyan. The foreign paymasters promised to support their Luktanon representatives to make inroads into the tribes, their future support being linked to evidence of results. Many within these groups arrogantly dismissed the work already done among the Mangyan. Often they did not investigate who was already working in these areas, neither did they have any intention of working together with other churches.

Buhid leaders were utterly bewildered to be told by one of these denominations that they had not received the Holy Spirit because they did not speak in tongues! These were sad reminders of the lack of unity between Christian churches, some of whom were on a crusade to build their own denominational empires by highlighting the supposedly spiritual shortcomings of what the Buhid believed and had been taught.

Other groups too maintained that the baptism the Buhid had received was insufficient, and that to be saved, they ought to be re-baptised into their own church. It was really disappointing to learn these attitudes, making it more difficult to welcome fellowship with these other parts of the Church, and in so doing, gain an enrichening from the differing emphases held by the denominations.

Such arrogance is lamentable, uttering condemnation when fellowship is genuinely being sought in a world that is already hostile to the Church, amidst a Luktanon society that despised the tribal. Buhid leaders want the wider fellowship with Filipino Christians and in a very few cases do enjoy such fellowship, but it is no wonder that Buhid are suspicious of the motives and attitudes of other brothers in the faith when greeted with such insensitive (and unbiblical) opinions.

Far from wanting to keep the Buhid in isolation from the wider Church, we encouraged them to seek and to accept fellowship cautiously with anyone who believes Christ is Lord. Despite criticism, we encouraged them to desire more of the Spirit of God, just as we ourselves recognised our own need not to become complacent with our limited experience of God.

Fearing their funds would be cut off if they did not report conversions within the first year to meet the quotas set for them by their absent paymasters, the Luktanon pastors targeted the established churches, re-baptising those who were willing to leave the Mangyan tribal church to join their denomination. The Luktanon pastors sent photographs back to the States and Korea recording this wonderful turning to the Lord. This ensured further investment. Re-baptising was not a problem for many Mangyan, as they gained materially from changing allegiances from being a poor, independent tribal church to becoming a denomination with wealthy foreign sponsors. They gained from having a concrete church building with a corrugated iron roof that was low in maintenance and high in prestige. Better still, rarely did they give a peso towards its construction. Funds became available, not only for the lowland pastor, but for the Mangyan to be trained, or for his services to be hired to carry out an evangelistic campaign.

There was the rub with the Buhid Church – could OMF not provide a similar scheme?

OMF determined that the building of the Kingdom should be born out of a compelling passion to share Christ with the lost, through prayer and not through offers of free land plots and free sacks of rice to join a particular church. After its forced withdrawal from China, OMF observed that the churches which survived and blossomed were not the ones where foreign funds had been poured in, but where the Chinese leadership had already been self-supporting. This confirmed the mission to exercise financial caution.

For a time, the Buhid resisted the sweet overtures of these denominations. Their passion was still focused on Christ, jealous to see His Kingdom advanced and further established. However, an occasional member was lured away by the promise of self-advancement and sometimes through spiritual motivation too, transferring churches to gain a scholarship to study at the denomination's Bible college.

* * *

All of a sudden the problem of how to disciple Baliya Fontan was resolved. Without any discussion and deliberations from either myself or the other churches, members of the Siyangi church, the church committed to twice-daily Bible studies and prayer, responded to the need by making trips five hours upriver to Baliya Fontan. They did not have to be coerced into taking their turn to go, but rather were so curious about the reports of the sudden and amazing birth of this church that many wanted to go and see for themselves.

Buhadan spoke about relocating there, and together with his wife, spent weeks at Baliya Fontan during the long school holidays, grounding the new converts in the faith. But they had school-aged children and if they remained there, it presented their children with a seven-hour walk and a half-hour jeepney ride to reach the nearest high school.

Buhadan's sister, Banglad, and her husband, Sulmay, were so thrilled by what was going on that they built a temporary house in Baliya Fontan for the dry season and were loaned land, without charge, to farm. Banglad taught them how to sing "like Christians" as she put it, so unlike the familiar dark chanting to the spirits of the dead. Everyone enjoyed learning to praise God, and many gifts of food were brought to Banglad and Sulmay's house to encourage them to stay. This couple's children were young and didn't need to go to school, and so they stayed on after Buhadan moved back downriver to Siyangi at the start of the new school term. Later, Banglad and Sulmay decided too it was perhaps time to have a spell back home in Siyangi and attend to their fields there and see their relatives. They assured the new church they would be back.

When Banglad and Sulmay arrived in Siyangi, the charred remains of their house confronted them. It had mysteriously burnt to the ground. Having lost everything, they adopted a very philosophical attitude, deciding that since God had allowed this to happen, and in view of their other house still standing in Baliya Fontan (albeit only a temporary dwelling), to return upriver, across the high mountain divide and establish themselves properly in Baliya Fontan.

I chanced to meet Sulmay in Bongabong market shortly before he was heading off to make his new home over in Occidental Mindoro province.

"Faduwasay – pray for us," entreated this man who normally was so shy that he rarely spoke with me. "Pray in particular that I will be able to answer more of the questions that the new believers ask!" His face shone with great sincerity.

Buhadan had remarked to me how Sulmay and he, and their

respective wives, worked as a team. The women led and trained the church with worship songs, whilst Buhadan concentrated on the Bible teaching. I had been curious enough to ask about Sulmay.

"Sulmay attends every session," replied Buhadan. "He sits there and nods his head, and because many of them there in Baliya Fontan are his relatives, they look to him for confirmation. When they look inquiringly, then Sulmay nods his head affirmatively, saying: 'that's true!'"

Although faced by a task of enormous proportions, Sulmay was surrendering to God in becoming an instrument the Almighty could use in building that church. I reminded myself of the unpromising material in the form of Anaw and Bado, the town fool-cum-comedian and the life and soul of the party, the two men of whom God had got hold and transformed. There were others too like Gano – the main elder whose illiteracy almost led the Manihala church into the clutches of a cult; Sayna – the one fascinated by time, detached from the other churches, who overwhelmed by the presence of God came out of his isolation and disinterest; or Anaw – the worldly politician, humbled and made small enough for the Lord to use. And what about men like Monay and Sagyom – Bible school trained, bowed in defeat of the aborted Datag Bonglay mission, who came back from out of the night of despair and warmed themselves by the fire of the Holy Spirit?

Many of these had at one time been like useless lumps of metal whom God did not discard. I noted He saw their unformed potential and fashioned them on His anvil and heated in the flames to become finely crafted fotols, fotols effectively wielded in God's hand in the Buhid Church.

Baliya Fontan had the real hope of becoming established through a young, untrained man with a growing hunger for God, made prayerful through his own devastating sense of incompetence.

The mango tree had fruited well.

ENGLISH-SPEAKING OMF CENTRES

AUSTRALIA: PO Box 849, Epping, NSW 2121.
Freecall 1800 227 154
e-mail: omf-australia@omf.net   *www.au.omf.org*

CANADA: 5759 Coopers Avenue, Mississauga ON, L4Z 1R9.
Toll free 1-888-657-8010
e-mail: omfcanada@omf.ca   *www.ca.omf.org*

HONG KONG: P.O. Box 70505, Kowloon Central Post Office,
Hong Kong.
e-mail: hk@omf.net   *www.omf.org.hk*

MALAYSIA: 3A Jalan Nipah, off Jalan Ampang, 55000, Kuala
Lumpur.
e-mail: my@omf.net   *www.omf.org*

NEW ZEALAND: P.O. Box 10–159, Auckland.
Tel 09-630 5778
e-mail: omfnz@compuserve.com   *www.omf.org*

PHILIPPINES: 900 Commonwealth Avenue, Diliman, 1101
Quezon City.
e-mail: ph-hc@omf.net   *www.omf.org*

SINGAPORE: 2 Cluny Road, Singapore 259570.
e-mail: sno@omf.net   *www.omf.org*

SOUTHERN AFRICA: PO Box 3080, Pinegowrie, 2123.
e-mail: za@omf.net   *www.za.omf.org*

UK: Station Approach, Borough Green, Sevenoaks, Kent, TN15 8BG.
Tel 01732 887299
e-mail: omf@omf.org.uk   *www.omf.org.uk*

USA: 10 West Dry Creek Circle, Littleton, CO 80120-4413.
Toll Free 1-800-422-5330
e-mail: omf@omf.org   *www.us.omf.org*

> *OMF International Headquarters:*
> *2 Cluny Road, Singapore 259570*